OIL PAINTING
TECHNIQUES

Geoff Stalker

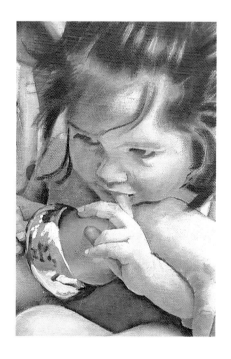

The Crowood Press

CONTENTS

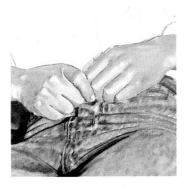

Contents

INTRODUCTION

I once watched a television game show where the question posed was 'Who invented oil painting?' The contestant answered 'Van Eyck' and according to the Quiz Master was credited with the right answer. They were both wrong, of course.

By the time Jan Van Eyck had painted the *Arnolfini Marriage* in 1434 there had been a couple of hundred years of experiments with various vegetable oils and solvents. It is true, however, that the *Arnolfini Marriage* is regarded as the first great masterpiece to be painted in oils. It was painted on an oak panel which had a ground of animal-skin and glue and chalk. The base for the pigment was linseed oil, which was a by-product of the linen industry and had been used in the making of furniture and in the polishing of musical instruments.

It is a painting that must have stunned fifteenth-century Flanders. It had a luminosity of colour that made frescos look pale and chalky by comparison. There were subtle gradations of tone and colour that could not be achieved with tempera because this new oil-based paint had a better covering quality. A slower drying time allowed Van Eyck to adjust and correct errors and work on details of unbelievable subtlety.

Van Eyck may also have been able to work direct from life in reasonable comfort. Tempera uses egg yolks as a base. You can imagine the smell of a studio with all those eggs and the expression on a sitter's face if one did a tempera portrait from life. The tempera paint you find in the shops nowadays is odourless and much more socially acceptable.

Van Eyck had used a tempera technique, painting on a white background, building up the pigment with layers of progressively darker paint. He used the same thin sable brushes that are used for tempera but the oil paint was less glutinous and flowed off the brush easily and consistently.

A few years later, in Italy, Pierro Della Francesca was using both tempera and oil on the same paintings. Whether this has been the cause of some of the deterioration of the paintings such as *The Baptism of Christ*, I don't know, but it gives some indication as to how experimental and adventurous the Renaissance artists were.

I could say that the first lesson of this book is not to mix oil painting with tempera, at least not until you really understand the substance. However, a more important lesson is to experiment.

The painters of the high Renaissance had a choice of three types of paint: fresco, tempera and oils. Each brought its own set of aesthetic limitations. Fresco was a method of applying water-based pigment on to wet plaster. A team of assistants would lay up just enough plaster on a wall for the artist to paint in one day. Next day another section of plaster and another day's painting; and so on until the wall and the painting were complete. The colours were pale and chalky and because the work had to be conceived in sections there had to be meticulous planning, a strong emphasis on preparatory drawing and no room for deviation from the original idea. Some of the great wonders of western civilization were executed in fresco; Giotto's *Arena Chapel* and Michelangelo's *Sistine Chapel* spring im-

Oil paint is simply ground pigment mixed with an oil-based solvent.

mediately to mind. If you can afford a team of assistants and like to paint on the grand scale, then take up fresco painting.

Tempera was the medium used for medieval book illustrations and early Renaissance religious icons, tabernacles and altar-pieces. Sometimes tempera was combined with gold leaf and lapidary work. Meticulous preparation was required from assistants: a glass-smooth plaster ground, preparatory drawings, paints ground and mixed with egg yolk fresh every day. The paint was applied in thin flat layers; soft gradations from light to dark or one colour to another were difficult to achieve because of the uneven consistency of the egg base.

And then along came oil paint. A medium that allowed you to paint without the linear constraints of preparatory drawing, allowed you to overpaint or sand down any mistakes, allowed you to paint any size on virtually any surface, even a flexible one like canvas. If you painted in oil, you did not need a team of assistants; you could do it all on your own, in private, in secret; you could cheat!

Oil paint was more than just a better kind of paint for prettier pictures; it was a medium that allowed artists to change, develop and adapt their ideas as they worked. This, together with the invention of the printing press and the telescope, triggered a release of the human spirit and imagination that spread beyond the realm of the arts to the world of science and letters.

When Titian painted the *Death of Acteon* or Rembrandt painted a self-portrait in oils, the paint was not just used to create an illusion, the substance of the paint was used to act as a metaphor for the imagined world or the real world. You could do anything with oil paints.

I hope that this book will encourage you to try a few of the techniques,

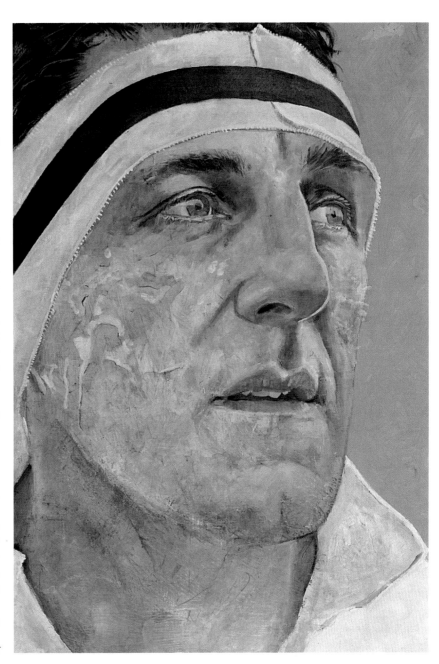

'Wade Dooley'. Whatever illusion you are trying to create with oil paint, you must bear in mind that it is only paint on a canvas. No more, no less.

tricks, short cuts and sleights of hand that I describe. I hope that some of the disciplines that I explain and the exercises I give you to try will help you to paint with greater technical facility and a more confident vision.

Above all, I hope that this book will trigger a release of your own spirit and imagination, and give you the incentive, and the confidence, to experiment with your own ideas and broaden your artistic horizons.

MATERIALS & EQUIPMENT

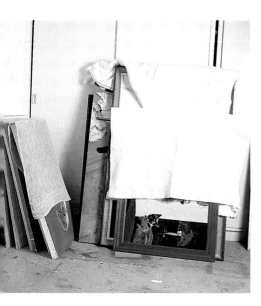

Either sell your paintings, store them safely or paint over them. Don't leave them around for future art historians to discover.

Your studio should be kept reasonably tidy and the floor swept at least once a month.

At the end of each session of work, clean your brushes and tidy up your paints.

The first, most important thing that you need is a place to work, whether this is the loft, the garage, or a separate room in the house. Wherever it is, it must lock out family, neighbours, dog and give you some important un-interrupted time.

This room should be equipped to fit your own needs. Do not feel that in order to paint you have to have a professionally equipped studio with large, north-facing windows and a resident nude in the corner by the door. An under-equipped studio is a necessary psychological scapegoat on those days when things go wrong.

There is a saying in sport, 'You have either got the gear, or you are good.' We have all seen the village cricketer with freshly ironed whites, brand new pads and gloves, the most expensive test-match bat, and perhaps even a helmet, being bowled for a duck by someone in a white T-shirt, and string for shoelaces. So, get what you can afford, but do not spend to excess. The history of art is peppered with examples of how the limitations and strictures an artist encounters can be the most powerful stimuli.

However you organize your room, there are a few safety aspects to be taken into consideration. Oil paint, turpentine, white spirit, linseed oi

> ## MATERIALS & EQUIPMENT
>
> - Oil paints
> - Canvas or paper, or any material with a suitable surface
> - A range of brushes (hog's hair, nylon or sable)
> - Sponges, rags, spray can
> - Easel, or other suitable support
> - Solvent and cleaner

Nail your picture to the wall using left-over timber and some adhesive cushion pads.

and all the new solvents are inflammable. A bottle of turpentine left in direct sunlight over the weekend is a fire hazard; so is an oil-soaked rag left too close to the fire.

A simple rule of thumb is to be reasonably tidy. I know that artists are not supposed to be tidy and that there are no references, in Vasari or Van Gogh's letters, to any artist ever sweeping up at the end of a hard day slaving over an easel. However, do make sure that all your bottles and containers are labelled and stored in a cupboard. Any inflammable material that is not

Store everything out of harm's way.

in immediate use should be stored in the shed or garage.

If you have young children, remember that tubes of paint look like a cross between toothpaste and a tube of sweets, so keep things out of their reach.

If you have any doubts or worries refer to a very good booklet 'Fire Safety Guide to the Home'. Your local post office or fire station will send you a copy on request.

Buying Materials

Artists' materials shops are part of a multi-million pound industry. The big manufacturers have done their market research and they know exactly who to target and where the most profit lies. They make their money by having lots of small outlets selling small amounts of goods to a lot of people. Most small towns have an art shop or a stationer's with an artists' materials section. They have a very small range of materials and a particularly narrow range of brushes and paints. In many of these shops, there is rarely a knowledgeable, experienced person from whom you can seek advice and assistance. Only in major cities are you likely to find a proper art shop. It may be worth while making contact with the local art college. They usually have a good students' shop and would welcome your custom.

Be very careful in the good art shops, though. They are very seductive places: all those beautiful rows of colours neatly laid out, those lovely untouched, unsqueezed tubes of paint. You only find out when you go to the counter that different colours of the same size paint can vary in price from a few pence to several pounds. You will save money if you get all the colour catalogues and price

A jar full of turpentine will act as a lens; in direct sunlight, this is a recipe for a fire.

lists and sit down for an hour or so. Read the small print and plan your palette according to your pocket.

Do not buy your paints in pretty wooden boxes. They are very expensive packages that will only clutter up your studio.

Paint

You can buy ready-mixed paint in tubes or cans. Cans are only of use if you paint very large canvases, often. I can never remember to put the lid

Tubes of paint are particularly dangerous when children are around.

Materials & Equipment

There are several whites available: Flake White is quick drying; Titanium White is the most opaque and perhaps the whitest; Zinc White is best for glazes but it is very slow to dry.

on securely, and I am always contaminating them with small amounts of other colours.

Mixing your own paints with powder paint and a binding medium was good enough for Rembrandt so it should be good enough for us. It can lead to a richer, more luminous palette if you are good at it. It is a lot of fuss and bother, but then it can be satisfying.

As a general rule, you will need as much white paint by volume as all the other colours put together. There are several whites available: Flake White is quick drying; Titanium White is the most opaque and perhaps the whitest; Zinc White is best for glazes but is very slow to dry.

Make note of the fact that most manufacturers produce two classes of paint, 'Artists'' colours and 'Student' colours. Artists' colours are, in general, more intense pigments and there is a range of about 100 or so different colours. The 'Student colours' have only about fifty colours and they mix less strongly with white paint.

Some text books tell you that, in theory, you can mix all the colours

you need with the three primaries, red, yellow and blue, plus black and white. Others advise using each of the colours of the spectrum plus black and white. The truth is that if you are a really top-class artist and a colourist of great sensitivity, you can get away with a limited palette range. Mere mortals need more help.

To create a balanced palette, you will need basic colours, of which there are several variations (*see* opposite for my suggestions).

Binding Agents and Solvents

Linseed Oil   This will improve the flow of colours. There are several linseed oils: refined linseed oil dries slowly; sun-bleached or drying linseed oil speeds up the drying process, which is useful when using glazes.

Poppy Oil   This serves the same purpose as linseed oil, but has a slightly different feel to it.

(Each of the above can be mixed with turpentine or white spirit.)

Oil of Spike Lavender   This can be used as a slower-drying turpentine.

You can also use various proprietary brands of artists' media which can make your paint dry gloss, matt or opalescent. They change the body of the paint.

In the last twenty years several alternatives to linseed oil and turpentine have been developed. Each has its own particular qualities and you should try them out to find which one suits your needs.

Pigments are made from ground minerals and metal oxides as well as synthetic chemicals with exotic names like Ferriferrocyanide, Cobaltinitrite, Phthalocyanine, Astraphloxine, Sulphoselenide and Dihydroxyamthaquinone.

Liquin   This is good for thin glazes and dries quickly.

Oleopasto   This can be mixed with paint to give texture to your brushwork and for building up thick layers of colour.

Wingel   This is a sort of gloss half way between liquin and oleopasto.

(All three are particularly good for mixing with translucent colours.)

Exercise

Paint a picture where each element of the work has a definable outline. Within the outline, paint each different object using a different binding agent as a base. Each image will have a different painted quality and a different surface. If the exercise turns out to be a good picture, you can then unify the whole with a glaze or binding agent.

A Balanced Palette

- A lemon Yellow
- Chrome Yellow
- Cadmium Yellow
- Indian Yellow
- Naples Yellow
- Jaune Brilliant
- Yellow Ochre
- Cadmium Orange or Chrome Orange
- Cadmium Red
- A scarlet
- A rose madder
- A crimson
- A violet
- A mauve
- A magenta
- Cobalt Blue

This palette should be adequate for most artists' needs. If you lay out your colours in the same order and the same pattern every time, and store your paints in the same order it will save you a lot of time in the long run. A boring exercise but a time-saving one.

- An ultramarine
- Prussian Blue
- Indigo
- Cerulean Blue
- Cadmium Green

- An emerald
- Viridian
- A turquoise
- Cinnabar
- Oxide of Chromium
- Olive Green
- Raw Sienna
- Burnt Sienna
- Raw Umber
- Burnt Umber
- Light Red
- A black (There are several blacks and dark greys.)

Buy Flesh Tint but do not use it to paint flesh with unless your sitter is very ill. Don't buy carmine, it's too expensive.

This is merely a suggested palette. One of the delights of painting is buying a few new colours and trying them out.

Supports and Surfaces

With oils you can paint on just about anything that doesn't move, wood, paper, metals as well as properly stretched canvases.

There is a range of easels, from the small portable to the huge studio easels that you can climb up. But you can get away with home-made structures of timber and nails on an old table. You can even just nail your canvas to the studio wall.

Applying the Paint

There is a vast range of brushes avail-able in different sizes and materials, such as hog's hair, nylon and sable. But you can also use sponges, rags, a spray can, or rollers, to apply paint; you can even paint direct from the tube.

Light and Ventilation

Natural light is best, of course, but if you have to work in the evening you can buy 'daylight' bulbs which give a good imitation of the real thing. An ordinary household light bulb gives off a warm light, deficient in blue and green, and you cannot compensate for it in your painting. This is why an evening's work always looks different in the cold light of morning.

Make sure that your workplace is well ventilated. Paints and solvents give off some noxious fumes, which won't poison you, but can cause headaches and chest problems.

Storage

You need somewhere dry to keep next week's new canvas and last week's masterpiece away from dust and splashes. A large cupboard set aside for the purpose is ideal, but a corner of the studio, where your work can be stood on end and covered, will suffice.

STRETCHING A CANVAS

Stretching a Canvas –
Step-by-Step (1–8)

Step 1   *Set all your materials and tools together: wood, hammer, mitre and saw, sandpaper, glue and a staple-gun. My staple-gun is a big heavy-duty one, using ½in (1.3cm) staples. It cost me a month's pocket money but it paid for itself after four canvases.*

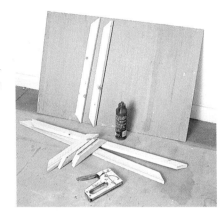

Step 2   *The stretchers are made from 2 × 1in (5 × 2.5cm) timber. If the stretcher is to be smaller than 18 sq.in (46cm) square, I use 1 × 1in (2.5 × 2.5cm). A hardboard support should be used unless you particularly want a drum-like quality to the surface of your work. The hardboard will support the canvas while you are working on it and will protect it from damage.*

Mitred corners are best, but not imperative. A stretcher longer than 18in (46cm) will need little diagonal cross-members to support the corners. Each joint should be very generously glued and stapled.

A properly stretched canvas, bough in a good art shop, is fine. All but the cheap and tatty ones are made from good materials. They do not warp, and as long as you keep knocking the pegs in and keep the canvas taut they will take any amount of working

Step 3   *Leave overnight on a flat surface, face down with a weight on each joint. Wipe off any excess glue with a damp rag. In the morning, sandpaper any rough edges.*

Step 4   *The canvas should be 6in (15.5cm) longer and wider than your stretcher. Sacking, corduroy, sailcloth, velvet, old curtains, as well as proper artist's canvas, all make interesting surfaces to paint on as long as they are properly stretched and primed.*

Step 5   *Staple middle to middle, top and bottom, left and right on the leading edge of your stretcher. Make sure that the warp and weft are in line with the edges. Then halve each distance making sure that you increase the 'pull' of your thumb and forefinger at each successive tack.*

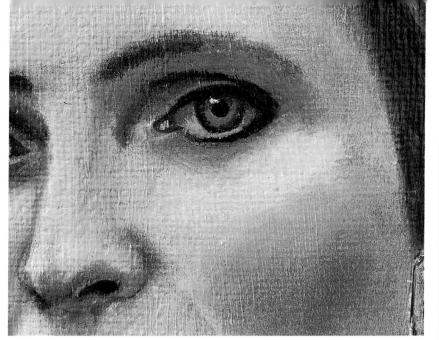

'HANNAH WARD-LEWIS' Well-primed raw hessian or sacking makes an excellent canvas.

and abuse. However, they are all made from the same kind of ready-primed canvas and are of the same, uniform weave.

Personally, I like to work on canvases larger than the ones readily available in the shops. Also, I like to experiment with all sorts of surface qualities and textures. Shop-bought canvas is fine, but it is usually unprotected. I make all my own canvases and stretchers, roughly sticking to the procedure described in the step by step guide.

'NICOLA' Corduroy also allows you to play around with textures and half-tones, as well as giving an interesting rhythm to your brush work.

Step 6 *When you have stapled it down, 1in (2.5cm) apart, your canvas should be taut. If you have done it properly, you will probably have blisters on your fingers. Tap in the staples with a hammer so that they lie flat with the canvas.*

Step 7 *Neatly fold each corner and tidy up the excess canvas on the back. Staple every 3in (7.5cm) or so.*

Step 8 *Tidy up the excess canvas, staple, and tap in flush with a hammer.*

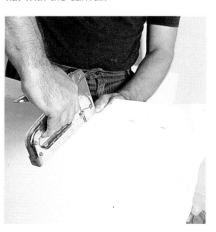

11

PREPARING A GROUND

There is a vast range of primers and undercoats, either specifically for oil painting or for general household use. Oil-primer, wood-primer and metal-primer as well as household emulsions and undercoats are all suitable as a base for oil painting. Only experiment and practice will give you the ground most suitable for your work.

The surface that you work on is a very important element in the aesthetics of your picture, so the number of coats of primer that you apply will depend on the finish you require: two or three coats of primer will still allow the texture of the material to play its part in your picture; six coats will give a smooth finish; ten coats will produce an extremely smooth finish, like the gessoes of Van Eyck.

Van Eyck used a mixture of animal skin glue and chalk. Titian used glue and gypsum. El Greco used a mixture of ochre, resin and glue; Vermeer, a pale-grey ground of chalk, lead white, umber and charcoal in an oil and glue emulsion. The French impressionists usually had a white or pale-coloured ground to increase the luminosity of their paint.

It is extremely important to sandpaper the surface between each application of primer, otherwise the paint will not key, and peeling may eventually result. Ensure that you prime the back and edges of a surface, before starting on the front.

Sandpaper between each coat of primer.

Alternatively, the palm of your hand is excellent since it forces the paint into the weave of the canvas and gives a smooth finish. You have to wash your hands anyway, so why waste a good brush?

You can apply primer with a brush, a sponge, a roller or a rag. For a very smooth finish, a sponge is ideal.

I found a piece of board, 6 × 4ft in an agricultural skip right next to the ditch I wanted to paint. I liked the irony of doing a painting on a found object in such circumstances. The board was covered in gobs of dried glue and the remnants of some textured wall-paper. It also had a series of eighth of an inch holes drilled into it. I had nothing to lose in this painting; if it didn't work I could blame the materials.

A couple of coats of emulsion primer was all the preparation I made. From then on it was a matter of fighting with the surface or utilizing it. I trowelled the paint on, almost sculpting the leaves and twigs. Doing the painting was a dirty, smelly struggle, but sometimes you have to create conflict for yourself, avoid the ideal, in order to get the best out of yourself.

Experiment

1. Divide your canvas into six sections and paint one area with one layer of primer, another with two layers, and so on up to the last area with six coats. Use this as a base for a painting and note the different effects the various preparations have on your painting.

Divide your canvas into six again and use three or four coats each of (a) oil-primer, (b) wood-primer, (c) metal-primer, (d) household undercoat, (e) matt emulsion, (f) vinyl emulsion. Again, note the different effects on the quality of both your finished painting and on your brushwork.

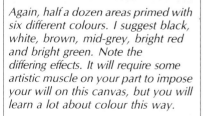

Again, half a dozen areas primed with six different colours. I suggest black, white, brown, mid-grey, bright red and bright green. Note the differing effects. It will require some artistic muscle on your part to impose your will on this canvas, but you will learn a lot about colour this way.

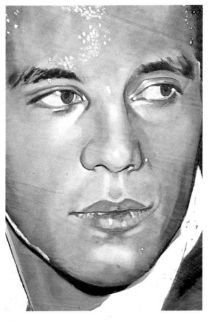

'JEREMY GUSCOTT'
Fine woven linen, sail cloth or cotton duck should be used when you need to pick out fine detail or subtle modulations of colour.

'MRS. SCOTT'
The smooth surface of hardboard can be used unprimed but it does tend to be very absorbent. A very smooth surface can be built up with three or four layers of primer, so that extremely fine detail can be worked up.

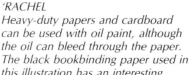

'RACHEL
Heavy-duty papers and cardboard can be used with oil paint, although the oil can bleed through the paper. The black bookbinding paper used in this illustration has an interesting texture and is excellent for dry-brushing or impasto techniques.

'GEOFFREY KENT'
Rough canvas with three or four layers of primer is ideal for painting flesh. Either dry-brushing complementary colours, mixing the pigment on the surface of the painting or layering glazes of transparent colour, the surface quality responds well.

'MARTIN OFFIAH'
The textured side of hardboard must be primed thoroughly. The little holes in the surface can be difficult to work with. With careful underpainting it can produce rich textures.

LIGHT AND COLOUR

Colour Theory and Colour Practice

I am on the horns of a dilemma when discussing colour. On the one hand I want to know everything about colour and what it does, and, on the other hand, when I sit down to work I want to do so with a sense of adventure. I want my work to be fluent, sparkling, even clever, and to do this I need to be in full command of my material. At the same time, I need to take risks, make mistakes, get lost occasionally; there should be a certain fear that stimulates the adrenalin.

Understanding colour is not learning the names of all the colours in all the tubes of paint; it is getting to grips with the basic principles of how colours react and interact. These basic principles should act as a kind of map to a very exciting and dangerous wilderness.

There is a lot of scientific information available to today's artists that was not available only 100 years ago to Monet and Van Gogh. At the end of the nineteenth century, Seurat and Signac were the first artists to take a scientific approach to painting. They studied the new science of optics and the development of photography. In

Lucien Pissarro made a note of Seurat's ideas in a beautifully concise and simple manner:

'The primary colours are red (1), yellow (2) and blue (3); the composite or binary colours are orange (1+2), green (2+3), violet (1+3). United, these colours produce the sensation of white, white light being the sum of all colours. Each colour serves as complementary to two others to form white light. As 1+2+3 are always required to form white light, the complementary of red (1) = (2+3) = yellow + blue = green complementary of yellow (2) = (1+3) = red + blue = violet complementary of blue (3) = (1+2) = red + yellow = orange and vice versa. According to the law of contrast, a colour achieves its maximum of intensity when brought close to its complementary. But while two complementaries enhance each other through juxtaposition, they destroy each other when mixed. Complementaries mixed in equal proportions produce grey. Two complementaries mixed in unequal proportions destroy each other partially and produce a broken colour which is a variety of grey, a tertiary colour. The law of complementaries permits a colour to be toned down or intensified without becoming dirty; while not touching the colour itself, one can pacify or neutralize it by changing the adjacent colours. If one juxtaposes in their pure state two equals of different degrees of energy, such as dark red and light red, one obtains (a) a contrast through the difference of intensity, and (b) a harmony through the similarity of tones. Two colours which do not go well together can be separated by an intermediary and unite them.'

their paintings they applied the prismatic colours in little dots. These coloured dots were applied according to the principle of 'simultaneous contrast': the fact that two adjacent colours mutually influence each other, each imposing on its neighbour its own complementary (the light one becoming lighter, the dark one becoming darker when they are of unequal value).

In order to work out what a particular colour's complementary was Seurat constructed for himself a colour wheel. On this disc he painted all the colours of the rainbow with some intermediate colours in between. His palette went from blue, natural ultramarine, artificial ultramarine, violet, purple, purple-red, carmine, red, vermilion, minium, orange, orange

Exercise

Painting a colour wheel is like practising scales on a piano; it is only of value if you do it with enthusiasm.

Allowing for Seurat's vague names for his colours you could construct a colour wheel for yourself. There are several ways of doing it. The one I advise is not particularly precise, either optically or chromatically, but it is very practically related to the tubes of colours you are likely to have in your box.

Paint several wheels. They are simple things with the basic colour laid out on the outer ring. These colours are modified with increasing touches of their opposite colour. Paint one by mixing the colour on the palette and applying to a smooth canvas.

In a second one, you can modify the colours by applying transparent glazes of the opposite colour with increasing intensity.

A third one can be painted on a coarse-textured canvas and the modifications made either by 'drybrushing' thick paint to the ridges of the canvas or by filling in the valleys with glazes of transparent paint.

yellow, yellow, greenish yellow, yellow green, green, emerald green, very greenish blue, greenish cyanic blue, greenish blue, cyanic blue I and cyanic blue II leading back to blue and thus closing the circle. The pure hues were concentrated round the centre of the circle. The primaries were mixed with white towards the edge of the circle.

Exercise

Make a simplified version of the colour wheel in card. Put a nail or pin through the middle and spin the wheel. The colours will merge and dissolve into white.

Light and Colour

In this painting of the rugby player Dean Richards, the light performs a number of functions: it sets the mood of the portrait; it creates, through highlight and shadow, the shape of the head; and it gives structure to the composition.

White, representing sunlight, is used to pick out the facial features. The shadows on the shirt are picked out in blues and ochres. The shadows in the flesh of his face are purple and green, with touches of red.

Light

Light is a form of radiant energy. It travels in a wave motion. The human eye and brain perceives the different length of some of these waves as colour. Below 400 millimicrons (measurement of the wavelengths of light) are ultraviolet rays. Above 700 millimicrons are infrared rays. Between these two levels we get the visible spectrum or rainbow.

The colour that we see on an orange or an apple, its local colour, is not the property of the orange or apple, but of the light reflected from them. The orange absorbs all the other colours of the rainbow especially the blue and reflects only those wavelengths of light which the human eye sees as orange.

Exercise

Take some transparent coloured sweet-wrappers or coloured filters from a camera lens and see how black a peach will look through a turquoise wrapper, or see how luminous a lemon appears when seen through a yellow wrapper.

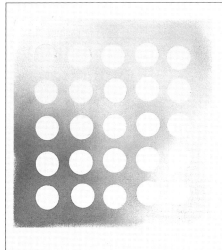

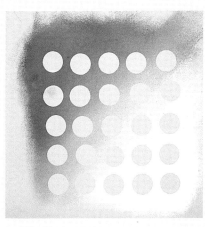

More Easy Exercises using Sticky Labels

1. Arrange a simple pattern of the labels on your canvas. Using either a brush or sponge apply the colour randomly before taking the labels away. In this illustration, the underpaint is photographer's mid-grey. Note how the grey is modified by its surrounding colour. You can do the same exercise with different coloured underpaint.

2. Same exercise, same pattern of sticky labels, but this time apply a range of grey from black to white. Note how the same photographer's mid-grey is modified by its surrounding tone and note also the illusion of space created.

Exercise

Thin yellow tissue paper stuck to the window pane gives a yellow cast to the lighter flesh tones, but it also has a profound effect on the other colours in the shadows. Set up a figure composition, preferably a nude, with light falling across the body. Put a plain-coloured curtain between the light source and half of the figure. Notice how the colour of the flesh changes.

In strong directional light the most exciting colour is to be found where the highlight meets the shadow, either gradually as in the breasts, or starkly as in the knuckles and wrists.

Light and Colour

DAYLIGHT

Daylight varies in its wavelength composition according to the atmosphere, weather and time of day. Monet, in his wonderful series of paintings of Rouen Cathedral, haystacks, poplar trees, and so on, spoke eloquently about the variations of light and colour. In the Rouen Cathedral series, we see twenty-five paintings of the same western façade at different times of the day in different light. The viewpoint is exactly the same and the composition varies only slightly, but with an astonishing freshness of colour. Each painting stands on its own.

I can think of no better task for anyone who wishes to get to grips with the intricacies of colour than to paint the view from their studio as often as time will allow. The more mundane the view the better, for putting aside 'composition' or the attempt to 'paint a picture' will focus the mind on the delights of light and colour.

Exercise

Put a red cloth over one lampshade and a green cloth over another. Shine both the lights on a bottle of milk or some other white object. The shadow of the red light will be green and the shadow of the green light will be red. Set up a still life, a figure in white clothes and play about with two or three different-coloured light sources. Focus the attention of your painting on the interplay of the different-coloured shadows.

It is interesting to note in the history of art, how many of the great masters utilized only one kind of light source throughout their paintings. Vermeer used daylight entering a room through a window, usually the left side of the room; Rembrandt often used artificial light, a candle or lamp within the picture, as did Joseph Wright of Derby. Turner's whole life was devoted to sunlight in its various forms.

ARTIFICIAL LIGHT

A photographic flash, a streetlight, a candle, the glow of a coal fire, emit light with a different mixture of wavelengths. The brain, however, has a mechanism for adapting and we can perceive all these light sources as the same. This mechanism has had artists in trouble for centuries.

The primary colours of emitted light are red, blue and green. The image on your television screen is transmitted by means of red, blue and green dots. The primary colours of reflected light, e.g. oil paint, are red, blue and yellow. When lights are mixed the result is increased brightness. When paints are mixed the colours are darker.

Emitted wavelengths are additive. Reflected wavelengths are subtractive.

Projecting colours and patterns on to a face or figure is a fun exercise, but it may also lead to a greater understanding of the relationship between colour, pattern, texture and form; particularly if it is the stimulus for a painting. Projected lights are insubstantial things, whereas oil paint is real and tactile.

Exercise

Repeat the exercise above with a human face. Use the different-coloured lights to bring out the shadows of the head, but more importantly to bring out the character of the sitter. Restrict the portrait to a very limited palette of the colours of your lights and their complementaries.

Experiment with projectors. As well as using different colours, use pattern and texture to distort the appearance of the figure.

Light and Colour

Colour Theory and the science of optics is a huge and fascinating subject. It can be the starting point and stimulus for so many paintings. I have merely touched on the subject.

So you are sitting there in front of your canvas, brush poised. How does it help you? You will only really start understanding colour when you get down to some real work; when you see that Yellow Ochre mixed with carmine gives a different effect from a glaze of carmine painted over Yellow Ochre. Different still is the effect of a delicate brush stroke of Yellow Ochre over a carmine ground.

Warm Colour, Cold Colour

Joshua Reynolds once gave a lecture to the Royal Academy about warm colours and cold colours and their relationship to space and depth perception in a landscape. Brutally trans-

cribed, he said that cold colours should be used for the background and warm colours for the foreground.

The cold colours are the greens, blues and purples; the warm colours are the reds, yellows and oranges. By describing colours as warm or cold, you can separate the 400 millimicron colours from the 700 millimicron colours.

Popular legend has it that Gainsborough painted *The Blue Boy* to confound his great rival, Reynolds. The foreground has a young boy in a sky-blue silk suit set against a brown landscape background.

The contrast in line and tone between the foreground and the background establishes spatial values. The blue foreground and red background work contrary to Reynolds' theories.

What Reynolds had said about warm colours in the foreground and cold colours in the background has some validity. Distant, heather-clad hills

do appear blue because particles in the atmosphere, particularly a damp British atmosphere, absorb colours at the red end of the spectrum, leaving only the blue end for our eyes to perceive.

If Reynolds was right, Gainsborough was even more right. In art, rules are made to be broken. A painting is to be judged not on how it fulfills the laws of colour theory, but whether it works as art.

Exercise

Paint two paintings of the same scene or seascape, one using cold colours for the background. Then do a second one, perhaps a sunset scene when you use cold colours for the foreground set against a vivid red and yellow sky.

The warm colours of the corrugated metal sheeting bring this dilapidated old shed right up to the picture plane.

The cold blues of the snow in the foreground and the reds of the sunset work contrary to Reynolds' theories.

Attention is paid to the edges of the log and the log root to accentuate space. Little touches of transparent mauve and Indian Yellow are applied.

Connor's Ditch – Step-by-Step

Connor's Ditch has three elements to it. For the logs and lily pads above the water, I mixed my paint with oleopasto so that I could build up the textures.

The shadows of the logs and leaves allow you to see into the water. I mixed my paint with wingel which allowed me to build up luminous colours with glazes.

The surface of the water changes from the top of the picture being completely reflective (showing the sky and the passing cloud), to being semi-reflective in the middle, to being totally transparent at the bottom. This gradual change, the interaction of reflection and refraction, and the influence of angle of vision is the substance of the picture. I used a little linseed oil and turpentine to mix with my paint. The canvas texture allowed me to create a gradual change, using rags to rub the paint into the grain of the cloth, and sandpaper to rub down the ridges of the canvas and the paint.

Once the paint is dry, subtle changes of tone and colour can be created by using a dry brush. I used an old brush and stained the bristles or hairs with the slightest smudge of paint. I then wiped off the excess paint and gently touched up the painting.

Step 1   *First, the basic tones are applied. The drawing is simple and is related more to the three elements than to the structure of the logs and lily pads. Little attention is given to colour accuracy.*

Step 2   *The log is roughly painted in and the lily pads repainted several times, building up the paint texture, layer upon layer.*

Step 3   *The log root is built up using thick paint, lump upon lump, sculpting the paint in the various directions of the wood.*

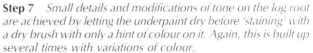

Step 4   In the shadows, transparent glazes of paint are built up in several layers.

Step 5   The sky reflected in the surface of the water is achieved by applying opaque blue (Cerulean, modified by a couple of other blues, plus Chrome Orange and white) with a rag, rubbing the pigment into the grain of the canvas.

Step 6   At this stage the paint is wiped away with a clean rag. This is done several times with slightly different colours to reveal the logs under the water. This is very much a trial-and-error method.

Step 7   Small details and modifications of tone on the log root are achieved by letting the underpaint dry before 'staining' with a dry brush with only a hint of colour on it. Again, this is built up several times with variations of colour.

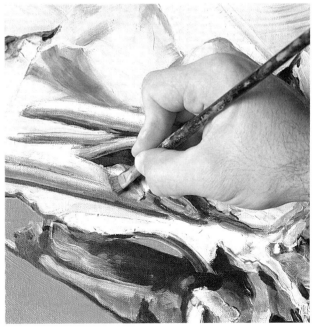

PAINTING PEOPLE

Portraits

When you first sit down to paint somebody, there is that same confrontational charge that exists when two competing sportsmen face each other, 'stare each other out', before a match. Who will prove to have the stronger will? How will fate balance you up? The business of staring at someone, and of being stared at, has its roots somewhere back in time and the jungle. For me, painting a portrait is the ultimate artistic test, not the pursuit of a likeness, for that is easy, but the pursuit of truth in another human being. How will I get through this person's many disguises and find out not just what they are like, but what they are?

You do this by treating them with respect, whether they are paying for the portrait or not. They do not want to come into your studio in their best clothes and sit down on the wet paint splashes of last week's picture. Clean your room a bit, put some music on and help them to feel relaxed.

Your initial drawings should not necessarily be in pursuit of a likeness or, indeed, structure, but an excuse to do some serious looking and staring. Only about 10 per cent of the surface area of a portrait consists of head or hands; the rest is clothes and background. Do not feel too proud to take photographs of the clothes to save your sitter's time as well as your own.

Remember that even the most experienced model can pose for an hour at most. I was once asked to paint a very nice lady, who could only hold a pose for about ten minutes. She had a cast in one eye and to all intents and purposes was cross-eyed. I thought that the best way I could paint her was to put one half of her face in shadow; however, she was a little overweight and the heavy sha-

dows emphasized her double chin. Deep into the sitting, as she grew tired, her shoulders drooped and she sank deeper and deeper into her chair. I scrapped the picture and started again. I accepted everything that she was, fat and cross-eyed, and she posed for ten minutes at a time, wide awake, full of life, and in her own way very lovely. The biggest insult you can pay anyone is to flatter them in a portrait.

One of the fundamental laws of human nature is that men are more vain than women. A man may have a face like a King Edward potato but he will ask you to note how large his biceps are and you had better not paint any grey hairs. A woman does not mind how you paint her as long as you don't try to look too deep.

One of the great battle-cries of modern portraiture is 'a portrait must

'HANNAH WARD-LEWIS I'
'HANNAH WARD-LEWIS II'
It often helps to paint a person in two totally different ways, particularly if you can't quite get through their 'disguises'. Put them in extreme situations or use totally different settings. Something will turn up!

If your portrait is destined to be hung in a particular setting, try and harmonize the quality of light of that setting with the light in your portrait. For example, if the painting is to be hung near a window on the left, make sure that the light source in your painting is from the left.

be a work of art first and a portrait second'. This is very true, but I am afraid that it has been used to justify some appalling work.

Portraiture has its own aesthetic values. When Rubens, who was a master of the grand composition, went home to paint his own family, we see only the standard 'head and shoulders in a rectangle' composition. And yet these simple portraits such as *Isabella Brant* or *Helene Fourment* are among the greatest works of art.

'WADE DOOLEY II'
Put your sitters in a pose which is natural to them, or brings information or context to your painting.

'THE ROBERTS'
Make sure that your studio is clean before your sitter arrives, especially since most people like to be painted wearing their best clothes.

Painting People

Quite a lot of good painters do have a genuine fear of portraiture, of the ability to achieve a likeness. In his letters to his brother Theo, even Van Gogh expressed constant reservations about getting a likeness.

The best way of getting over this fear is to have a regular model or sitter; either someone you pay or someone you love. This sitter should be instructed never to criticize, should pay compliments on a regular basis and never make suggestions about how the work can be improved. After the third or fourth portrait, you will start looking for and finding all sorts of new and interesting aspects.

After the tenth portrait you will learn that a portrait starts with a likeness and moves on, rather than ends when the initial likeness has been achieved.

'RACHEL AND WILLIAM'
Painting children is extremely difficult. Their faces change so rapidly from week to week and their mood from moment to moment. Often their parents don't know what they want from a portrait; sometimes they should have sent them to a photographer instead. They never keep still and you can never get anyone's attention, parent or child. Playing peek-a-boo behind the canvas ensured that I got a constant, startled expression from the little boy.

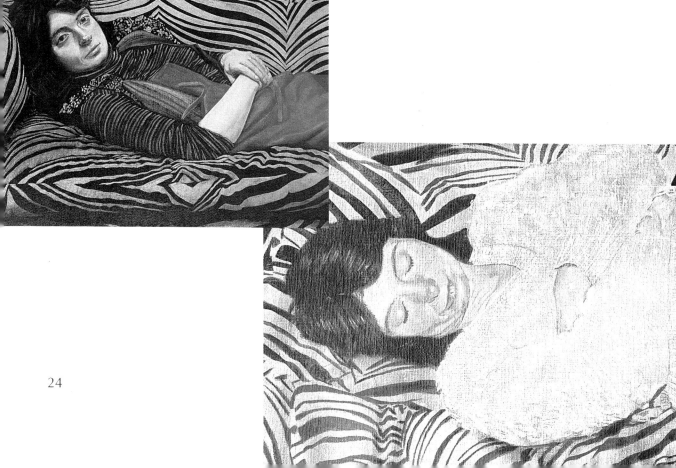

Flesh Tones

You may have in your box of paints a colour called Flesh Tint. It is nothing of the sort. Do not use it in portraits unless you want your sitter to look like a very sick tailor's dummy.

I do not have a ready-made formula for mixing flesh colours, apart from the fact that flesh varies greatly from person to person, and that the prevailing light conditions will affect the skin colour. More than this, however, the colours of the flesh in a portrait have to balance with the colours in the rest of the painting.

However there are two useful guides to getting the right tones and hues.

The first is a simple one of choosing two colours from opposite ends of your colour wheel and mixing them in differing ratios. Mix these resultant colours with various amounts of white.

The second approach is a tonal one. Set out a palette of five very dark colours which include a red, a green, a blue, a purple and a brown. Mix five more mid-tone colours, five light colours and five pastel colours. In the initial part of the painting, mix colours of the same tone only; these will give you flesh tones close to those you need.

On a separate palette mix in various ratios Indian Yellow, Alizarin Crim-

When working in this 'tonal' manner it is advisable, after you have mixed and laid out your palette, that you use a different palette for each separate tone. Once you have got the groundwork done on your picture, you can then start mixing things up as you begin to modulate your tones, and work in details.

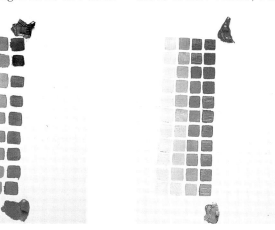

A tonal approach to mixing flesh colours. Choose two colours from the opposite ends of the spectrum (see your colour wheel). Mix gradually from one colour to the next, then repeat with the addition of varying amounts of white.

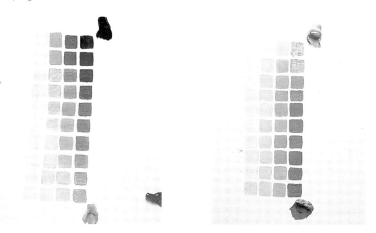

son, brown-pink, ultramarine and Phthalocyanine Green. Thinned out with a lot of liquin or linseed oil, use a glaze to balance the colours.

These little exercises can be more than just a way of discovering flesh tones. They are the doorway to a whole range of colours and tones. As a musician practises scales, an artist should practise mixing colours. Two colours and white is all you need. Later on you can introduce a third colour instead of white, just to see what happens.

Painting People

Transparent and Opaque Colours

Some pigments are made from crushed minerals, some from vegetable matter; others are strange metal oxides cooked up in Quatermass's laboratory. You do not need to know which, but you do need to know that they vary in intensity. Only practice will teach you which ones you need to mix with a trowel and which ones are so powerful that you need only a tiny drop. You also need to know that some paints can be mixed with linseed oil or liquin or some other binding agent to be used as a glaze or transparent coloured film. Other paints are not suitable as glazes but are good for impasto work.

Exercise

Using a white-primed board, set up a very light still life or figure. Arrange a palette using transparent colours. I suggest Indian Yellow, mauve, Olive Green, Cinnabar, Ultramarine, Purple Madder, alizarin. Do not use white because you will be utilizing the white of your board or canvas. For black, use Indigo.

Using a glazing medium mixed with a little turpentine, build up your painting with thin washes of paint, colour by colour, tone by tone. Each successive glaze will alter the colour of the base and will also darken the tone. Keep each colour separate; do not mix them, and make sure that you clean your brushes between colours.

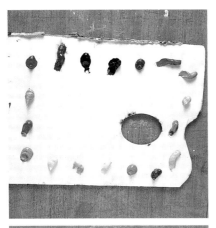

Once you have identified the opaque colours and the transparent colours in your tubes of paint, set out two separate palettes. Use both palettes by all means, but while you are working try to get a sense of how the paints feel on the end of your brush.

When mixing transparent colours for glazes, try and do it on a white palette. White formica or an old white ceramic tile will shine through the pigment and allow you to mix your glazes with more subtlety. Disposable paper palettes are excellent for glazing work also; it is vital that your palette is clean or your painting will pick up any ambient dirt.

Painting People

Permanent and Fugitive Colours

Direct sunlight will in time bleach most colours. Away from sunlight, some pigments will last for centuries. Others will change colour within a few years. There is a code on some tubes of paint to indicate permanence.

These two portraits of Rory Underwood, the rugby player and RAF pilot, were painted using different sets of paints. In the first I used a raw, opaque paint, building it up on a dark grey base.
In the second, I painted on a white base using linseed oil, liquin and turpentine, and transparent paints, building up the picture in layers of darker and darker paint. Highlights were then picked out in opaque, tinted whites.

Exercise

Arrange a dark, sombre scene. Take a heavily textured canvas or the back of hardboard, and prime with black or dark brown. Arrange a palette of opaque colours. I suggest Yellow Ochre, Vermilion, Cerulean Blue, Oxide of Chromium, Cobalt Blue, Violet, Raw Sienna and black and white. Build up in thick gobs of colour from very dark to white, making the most of the texture of your ground.

Exercise

Choose a rich, violent colour straight from the tube, an orange or a purple. Using black and white to modulate the tones, paint or sketch a portrait; you will end up with a rather ghastly likeness. Let the painting dry for a day or two before starting to do the real work. Using a full palette now try and rescue the portrait's colour value. You have a reasonable likeness, all you need to work on are the flesh tones and colours by balancing the yellows with the purples, the greens with the reds, and so on.
This painting was rescued from a layer of Ultramarine and Viridian underpainting.

27

Painting People

'GLEN SMITH'
The angle of view in a portrait addresses the same problems as a horizon does in a landscape painting. Looking down on a figure with the artist standing up and the subject sitting or lying down immediately puts the artist 'in command' of the social situation in the studio. This may or may not be conveyed through the painting. Conversely, putting the sitter higher up than the artist tells another story.

'JIM SHERA'
The window-ledge in this painting acts as a surrogate horizon, thus elevating the figure. The mace in the foreground helps to give the picture some depth as well as define what the picture is about. The cloak, the chain of office and the mace can be taken away and painted separately.

'THE FREEMASON'
You must also take into account where the sitter is in relation to surroundings and associated objects. Putting all the accoutrements of office in a picture may tell the world that the subject is a mayor, a freemason or a bricklayer. The odd chain or spirit level may be fun to paint, but do not let them take over the painting.

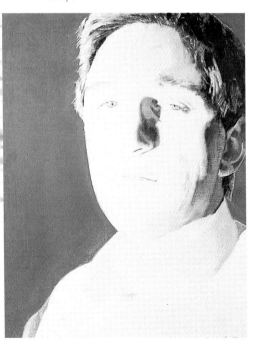

Angle of View

Think carefully about your composition, try out different angles, different poses, different settings, different lightings, but do not confuse slickness and experimentation with the real business of portraiture, the pursuit of truth in another human being.

Exercise

Put your subject in strong sunlight or project a strong light onto the face. Bleach out as much of the colour as possible and see if you can make a portrait with what little information there is left.

The Face

When painting or drawing a face, a good guideline is to take the distance between the pupils of the eyes as a constant measurement that you can compare with all other distances and angles.

Is the length of the nose from the bridge to the tip longer or shorter than the distance between the eyes? How does the angle of the line of the mouth compare with the angle of the line of the eyes?

Draw lines through the eyes through the bottom of the nose through the mouth and the bottom of the chin. How do these measurements compare with that constant of pupil to pupil?

Light can be your greatest ally in a portrait. Rembrandt used shafts of light as a metaphor for a halo. Physiognomical features such as nose, mouth or eyebrows take on a different aspect. Occasional characteristics of the face, a dimple, a mole, a broken nose, may disappear or be highlighted. You can also use light to break up the face of the figure, force a particular expression or as a compositional device to focus attention on a particular feature. The pure white area can also act as a key by which each other tone or colour can be related.

SPECTACLES

Glasses are easy to paint and with judicious use of highlights and reflections, they can be used as a major influence on your composition. The refractive and reflective qualities of the glass can be used as a disguise for the sitter.

One thing to note however is that people who wear glasses often use the top of the rim to shade their eyes from the light, so you often get a black shadow running along the line of the eyeball. You can use this to say a lot about the sitter. You can also use this to disguise any difficulties you may have in painting pupils and irises.

Exercise

Try and do a portrait of someone just using their spectacles. Ignore the rest of the head; just paint the frames and the eyes seen through the glass. See how much of the likeness or portrait you can get. As well as being a fun and quick thing to do, it can also give you an indication of how great a part eyes play in getting a likeness, and how influential 'eye contact', or the line of a sitter's gaze, is in the character of a portrait.

Exercise

Do the opposite of the above exercise. Paint everything but what is within the frame of the spectacles. Or if you wish, have the sitter wear dark glasses. This will allow you to focus all your attention on anatomical details such as the length of the nose compared with the width of the mouth.

These three portraits taken from the same large picture show different approaches to spectacles. The first shows how you can use them to focus attention and detail; the second shows how the distortions of the heavy glass give a playful touch to the gaze. The dark glasses in the third is the painter's soft option.

Painting People

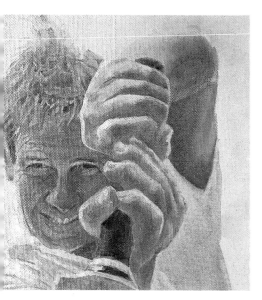

This cricketer had huge meat plates of hands. They had to be an integral part of his portrait.

Hands

Some people communicate more with their hands than they do with their mouth. In the Arab world hand gestures are a formalized adjunct to speech.

The history of portrait painting is full of wonderful hands, from the great gestures of Gericault, Delacroix and Rubens to the intimate little silences of Cezanne's *Woman at Prayer* or the gnarled care-worn fingers of Van Gogh's *Potato Eaters*.

You cannot avoid hands in a portrait or figure study. To have your sitter hide them out of the way or perhaps sit on them may solve a little painterly difficulty for you, but it may also convey something about the subject that is not true or that you do not wish to say. Worse still, it could convey something about you as a painter that is true!

They are such a complicated physical structure, made up of tubes and cubes and odd lumps, and the only real way for a painter to understand how they work is through regular and frequent life drawing and life painting.

Exercise 2

Put the hands in strong sunlight so that the knuckles and the veins stand out in strong chiaruscuro. Paint the shapes that the highlights and the shadows form.

Exercise 3

Paint one of your own hands in several positions; resting, holding something gently, holding something tightly. Put it beside a mirror and paint its reflection so that you do not just paint the left or right hand.

This is the right hand of a surgeon. It had been used to cut up so much living flesh.

Exercise 1

The first exercise is to put your paints away and hold the hand you wish to paint. Feel for the bones that make up the fingers and move the knuckles and joints around a bit. Feel the palm of the hand and try to form some picture of the structure of the ligaments, muscles and tendons. Touch the padded skin of the palms and then pick out the lines of the veins on the back of the hand. You can then start to try and paint this particular hand.

This perfectly manicured thumbnail just had to be picked out in profile.

Few things are deliberate in painting. Having difficulty painting this lively and energetic girl I had to get her mother to hold her still long enough to do some drawings. The hands then took over the picture.

Exercise 4

Place the hand on your canvas and draw an outline round it. This will help you avoid too much drawing and focus your attention on the colours and textures of the skin. Note the influence the skeleton of the hand has on the colour of the skin, particularly where bones are close to the surface. Covering the hand with a thin layer of paint and taking a palm print is another way of taking a short cut through the drawing stage.

These are the hands of Gee Armitage the jockey. Whether she was answering the phone, making tea or riding in the Grand National, her hands always worked as a neat symmetrical pair.

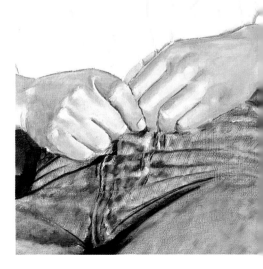

Painting People

Hair

Painting hair is one of those easy jobs that you save for when things are not going too well. A few flicks of the brush in roughly the right places and you can go to bed thinking that you are a genius.

You must however do the hard work of some preparatory under-painting, establishing the tonal values, creating the shape of the hair and mixing your colours accurately.

The manufacturers and colour chemists of hair dyes do not seem to understand that most hair is a complex mixture of several colours. It has subtle reflective qualities and areas of the deepest darkest shadows.

Using the hair to catch the light can be a major factor in the composition of your painting.

Using the hair to catch the light can be a major factor in the composition of your painting.
I usually paint in the darkest areas of the hair first, using a lightly loaded brush or sponge, rubbing the paint into the weave of the canvas. I then build up the shape of the hair with some careful drawing using a thin sable brush and thinned liquid paints. I let everything dry before I paint in the highlights with as many glints of colour and tone as I can see or get away with.

This woman's hair is not a natural colour; it picks up and reflects the colours of the surroundings. For the shadows, I put in a mixture of Burnt Sienna and Prussian Blue with a dry brush. There is some magenta and Emerald Green with a little Viridian. Some Flake White is laid on rather thickly for the highlights and the same brush is used to flick in some of the curls at the front of the hair.

In a portrait I always do the hair last, have lost count of the number c times sitters have had their hai cropped, permed, Afroed or dye when I am half-way through thei painting.

A person's hair is often a ver definite statement about themselves in a way that clothes cannot be. Hai can represent a battlefield of sel image versus fashion, greyness, co our and baldness. How this conflic is resolved can offer insights into sitter's character.

Painting People

This woman had hair all over the place. The curls and tresses danced about in wild abandon. Some Indigo and Blue Black were used in the deep shadows and the underpaint. The red tones were flicked in with gobs of Yellow Ochre, Naples Yellow and mauve. The highlights were Zinc White with a little Italian Pink. The brush work was rather free and the drawing may not have been very accurate, but the rhythm and the movement were.

Short cropped hair means painstaking work for the artist. Once you have done the underpainting in the appropriate tones and colours, tiny dabs of highlight are applied with the 'toe end' of a flat brush.

White hair is lovely to paint. The white highlights can be used as a 'halo' or to pick out the head in the overall composition. The shadows pick up and reflect all the colour in the surroundings.

33

Painting People

Eyes

Eyes are easy to paint, but very hard to paint well. We receive such subtle and intimate signals from them. The tiniest change in the angle of the gaze or the merest hint of a wrinkle in the corner of the eye can change the expression from angry to compliant, the mood from blissful to pained. I have painted so many eyes with painstaking care and got every measurement as accurate as a brush can render, to find in the end that the whole tone of the painting is wrong – accurate, but wrong.

At other times, I have slapped paint around for no particular reason and suddenly something jumps out of the picture and hits me over the head. So, these days my strategy is to have no strategy, my technique is not to have a technique. I just paint away as receptively as I can, for as long as it takes for the mood and expression to suggest itself. The painting will tell me when it is ready, when it is right. My job is to be there when it happens.

Part of the difficulty of painting eyes is that they are such sculptural forms, defined in linear terms and characterized by colour.

One approach is to use a fine pencil or ball-point pen and draw precisely the lines of the eyes, taking note of the detail such as the ⅛in-thick line

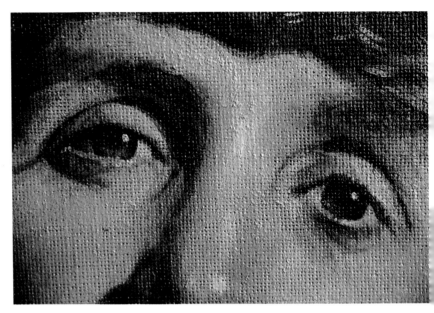

'SUE BARKLEY'
Even in a straight face-on portrait, the angle of the eyes can be used to effect. Eyes are asymmetrical and rather than being a problem for a painter, they should be a stimulus.

of pink eyelid, the little horseshoe in the corner of the eye, the wrinkles or bags under the eye. You can then paint in the colour, almost by numbers.

The second approach is to build up in paint, from the eyeball, the iris and the pupil, then sculpt the shape of the eyelids over the eyeball.

A third approach is to treat the eye as another part of the body, ignoring its psychological overtones. Just treat what you see as a collection of tones and colours.

> If someone is reading or looking intently at something near then the pupils will focus inwards, in other words they will be slightly cross-eyed. If someone is looking into the distance, or staring into space, you can treat the discs of the iris and pupil as parallel in direction.

> The skin changes colour quite significantly round the eyes. There are lots of blues, greens and purples to watch out for.

'SANDRA 4'
'The eyes on that portrait follow you round the room.' If the subject of a portrait is looking directly at the artist, the eyes of the sitter will look out of the picture.

The rough texture of the hessian canvas makes close detail difficult and linear expressions impossible, but the soft gradations of tone and the colour mixes that a textured surface can give you more than make up for it. The four highlights, the sharp one on the iris, the corner of the eye, the hollow of the eye and the bridge of the nose can express what you want to say about shape. The shape of the two triangles of 'white of eye' are all you need to convey expression.

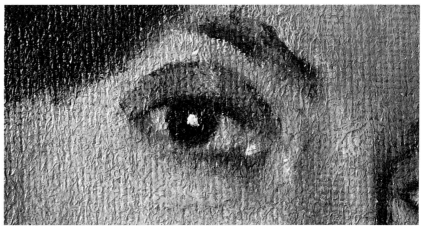

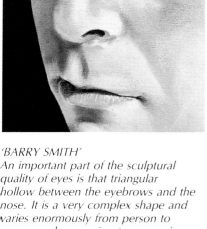

'BARRY SMITH'
An important part of the sculptural quality of eyes is that triangular hollow between the eyebrows and the nose. It is a very complex shape and varies enormously from person to person and expression to expression. Eyelashes are not just a decorative addition to the eyelids either; you can use them to break up the lines of the eyes and also to emphasize these lines.

This woman's eyes were of a ravishing blue colour. I liked the lines of her eyelashes, the crease of her eyelid and her eyebrow, but the most important aspect was the way her heavy lids came low over the pupils of her eyes.

The size of the pupils in relation to the size of the iris is governed by the amount of light available. In this 'Wade Dooley' painting I wanted to get across the same clarity of vision that an athlete experiences when the adrenalin is flowing. This involved pin-prick pupils, precise rendering of the reflection in the eyes and the odd little flecks of white detail around the eyelashes and in the little join between the eye and the lower lid.

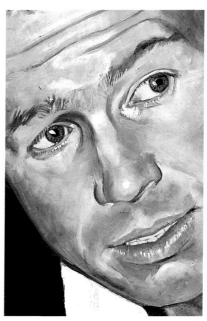

'RICHARD HILL'
The whites of the eyes are not white. They are a complex mixture of colours ranging from pink in the corner of the eye to paler blue round the iris. The tonal quality of the white of the eyes can be measured by comparisons with any white highlights and the pure black of the pupil. Highlights such as the reflections and the drops of dampness can be used not just as flashes of painterly skill but also as a means of bringing attention to the eyes. These highlights can be emphasized by a little ring of dark paint round the white.

Painting People

Dress

So many good portraits fail as good paintings either because too much attention is paid to the rendition of the shapes and patterns of clothes and fabrics or because, conversely, not enough attention is paid. Van Dyke and Rubens solved the problem by employing students and talented technicians to paint fabrics in for them.

Try to influence sitters' choice of dress by encouraging them to wear clothes that are 'paintable' but interesting. Discourage the choice of paisley blouses and pin-striped suits, the first for being too difficult and the second for being too dull to paint. And bear in mind that very fashionable clothes are usually out of fashion by the time a portrait is complete.

Clothes present opportunities as well as problems. The tartan shirt of this old man allowed me to use the stripes of the material and the undone button to define his belly and to say something about the sitter.

It was important to paint the primness of the pink, knitted pullover as a contrast to the high-tech background. This involved taking photographs and borrowing the garment for the duration; the highly detailed, stitch by stitch painting was more fun to paint than I thought it would be.

Exercise 1

Set up your easel opposite your wardrobe. Open the door and paint the contents as you find them.

Sometimes painting portraits is just letting the sitters speak for themselves; all you have to do is fill in the patterns and textures.

Regular patterns, such as the spots on the sitter's dress do not present too much of a problem as long as you draw them precisely in pencil beforehand, noting both angle and size; variation in tone can be rendered with thin glazes.

Exercise 2

Henry Moore, in his sculpture, showed us how drapery could be used to say much about the nature of the figure underneath. Arrange a nude, preferably reclining, and in turn drape three or four different sheets of fabric over the figure. Note how pattern affects the perception of the shapes underneath. Note the difference between a reflective material like silk and a plain white cotton sheet.

Family Portrait – Step-by-Step

I was commissioned to paint a large family in Michigan. The timing of the commission coincided with the writing of this book so I was persuaded to allow the photographer in several times during the course of its production, mistakes, warts and all.

The painting was not to be a portrait in the usual sense. I decided to break the picture down into four parts, each a separately stretched canvas with Jim, the father, included in each section. When he dies, each family will have their own section of the painting with father included. Ostensibly, it was to save any squabbling after the funeral, but in reality it gave me the opportunity to do four paintings of this remarkable man. The picture, when put together makes a whole of about 10ft (3m) by 5ft (1.5m).

The stretchers are made of 2 × 1in (5 × 2.5cm) timber, joined endways on with a hardboard panel. There are diagonal cross-members to strengthen each joint. This will limit any warping during transit.

The canvas is medium to fine woven raw cloth. There are two layers of mid-grey primer, each applied with a sponge. Finally there are two layers of drab green undercoat laid on with the palm of my hand. Apart from the fact that I had run out of sponges, I like the surface quality that this gives. Each layer had a light wipe over with medium-grade sandpaper.

I did not have enough easels, so I nailed the canvases to the wall using wooden battens and adhesive mirror pads. At this stage, I had only a vague idea of the composition. In theory, I should establish the background first, but my instincts told me that I needed to get a couple of foreground figures sketched in first, so that I could get in my mind where the picture plane is.

The painting is a social painting; it will perform a social function and is about the relationship of the old man with his progeny. The painting will succeed or fail, not on its 'painterly' values, important though these are, but on whether I have got the people right and in the right form. It is a matter of feel and instinct and insight. What talents a painter has in the way of colour, texture, sense of space, manual dexterity, tonal judgement or capacity for work; whatever painterly skills the painter has, they serve merely as the vocabulary, the grammar, the sentence structure for a much broader document, a longer essay. Getting the people right as well as getting the paint right is a matter of groping about in the dark and when you recognize that you have touched something worth holding onto, you grab tight and hang on.

Step 1 I started with the old man's head; it has a nice clean line to it. There is the occasional hint of Lime Green, Cobalt Blue and Mauve in the white base of the highlights. The paint was scumbled in using a worn ½in (12mm) flat sable brush. The main part of the face is a mixture of Crimson, Cerulean Blue, Indian Yellow and Italian Pink. There is the odd touch of Jaune Brilliant and Lemon Yellow, applied by mistake.

The spectacles at this stage were still the grey-green undercoat.

Step 2 I took a bit more care with the mother and daughter. I drew in the figures in coloured pencil. I needed to establish some sort of tonal range so I used Burnt Sienna with some Prussian Blue for the underpaint of the hair. The same gob of paint with another blue added was used for the underpainting of the swimsuit.

The baby's hat is Flake White with a lot of liquin to help it dry quickly. The same paint with a little Naples Yellow was used to sketch in the highlights of the hair. Some Burnt Umber, Italian Pink and a touch of Cerulean Blue with a little white added, made a poor basic flesh colour for the mother, so I cleaned it off with a dry rag, but luckily the grey/green showing through the residue of paint gave me a close approximation of what I wanted. I left well alone and used a mixture of lightly tinted whites (Mauve, Antwerp Blue, Viridian, Cadmium Yellow, Vermilion) for the highlights. I scumble in a little Cadmium Orange as an afterthought.

Step 3 I was a little careless with the underpainting of the two little girls and the young boy in the foreground. The tone was just about right but the flesh took on the colour of sticking plaster, and was a distraction when working on other figures. I returned to work on them earlier than was wise, and worked in a lot of detail such as hair and costume. This meant that I was committed to them in the composition; would I have the courage or time to paint them out at a later stage if necessary?

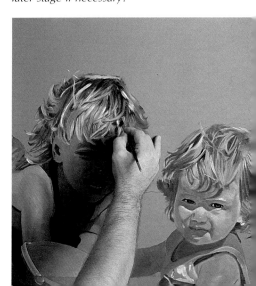

Step 4 *I needed a sky, I needed to establish an eye-level. I played around with various horizons. I reminded myself that they are separate canvases so the horizons and sky need not be uniform.*

Step 5 *The figures in the right-hand panel are sketched in. The flesh was too yellow in two of the figures. I could not bring myself to paint in the tartan of the old man's bermuda shorts; a matter of taste rather than technical difficulty.*

40

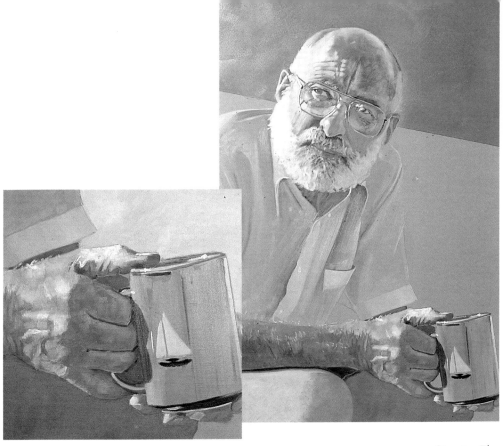

Step 6   The different light source
in the separate panel of the old man is
deliberate. I worked on him almost to
a conclusion. I paid a lot of attention
to the hand and its skin tone: some
Magenta, some Antwerp Blue and
Leaf Green in the shadows; very bold
white highlights. Half wiping the
white brush dry, I played about with
the half-dry paint on the forearm. I
accidentally got the effect of hair on
his arm. I developed this further in the
shadows.

Step 7   He has a good head. I worked
on it with a full palette of about fifty
colours. It would have been easy to go
into more detail, wrinkle after
wrinkle. The hard part is knowing
when to stop. The highlights on the
head are not pure white. I mixed a
reservoir of Titanium White and
added a touch of Jaune Brilliant and
Blue Mauve where necessary. I had
as much trouble with the sky on its own
as I had with the figure.

Step 8 *The boy is the right choice for the foreground, not just because of his personality but because the colour of his bright ginger hair with its yellow highlights brings him right forward to the picture plane. His tall sister is a much paler figure.*

Step 9 *I was convinced that the man with the dark beard in the extreme left was in disguise. I was tempted to tug his beard or his hair to see if they were wigs. Some Payne's Grey and Burnt Umber made up the underpaint for the hair. When it had dried, a few flicks of white and Naples Yellow, perhaps a few other colours, conveyed the odd grey hair and highlight. In spite of the fact that there was not much face to be seen, it was quite difficult. The colours in the shadows of his eyes and nose were very fugitive. Some Sap Green, Yellow Ochre, Cobalt Blue, Carmine; they are all in there somewhere. His nose has a rounded form and it was difficult to place the highlight.*

Step 10 *I reached a stage where some figures had been sketched in and others were almost complete. I needed to put the whole picture together, not so much to make the composition balance, but to use the completed figures as a key to finishing the sketched figures.*

There are some thought-out compositional links, like the reverse postures of the boy and the old man in the background, the splayed legs of the baby and the girl with the incongruous 'five chairs' on her T-shirt, but these are minor incidentals.

43

Painting People

Nudes

Oil paint is the perfect medium for painting nudes. No other paint gives you the range of colours, the range of textures, the directness of touch that oil paint affords you. You can – you must – use the paints to act not just as an illusion of naked flesh, but as a metaphor for it. The sensuous overtones of a brush dipped in oil paint and linseed oil serves as a constant reminder that what you have before you is flesh, not meat, a naked other person and not a plaster cast or a tailor's dummy.

There are four ways by which you can get to paint nudes.

You can go along to your local art college or evening class. The models will be experienced, you can pick up lots of advice from tutors and from fellow students, and it will be a good stimulating atmosphere.

You can persuade friends and family to pose for you. Although the models will not be able to pose for long periods, the intimacy of painting people you know and love will add to the experience and, it is hoped, the painting.

You can hire a model privately. There are model agencies in most big cities, but they can be very expensive and all the models tend to be of the same age and type of figure.

Finally, people may approach you and invite you to paint them in the nude.

For any figurative painter, life drawing and life painting are an absolute essential. It is not just the understanding of anatomy and what the body will do, although that is very important, it is that both physically and expressively the human body is the basic grammar of painting.

Having a nude in your own room or studio is not the same as going along to your local life class. There is bound to be an incongruous note set between a clothed artist and a naked model.

Sometimes the act of stripping away the disguises of clothes and make-up can lead to the most open of portraits.

44

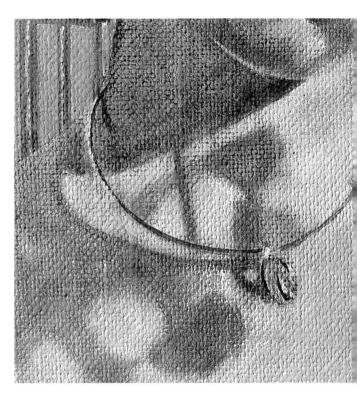

*One solitary article of clothing or jewellery can be used as a key or as a starting point to a number of experiments
in the painting of flesh. Shadows cast by flowers on the flesh as well as a necklace can be the focal point of a nude.*

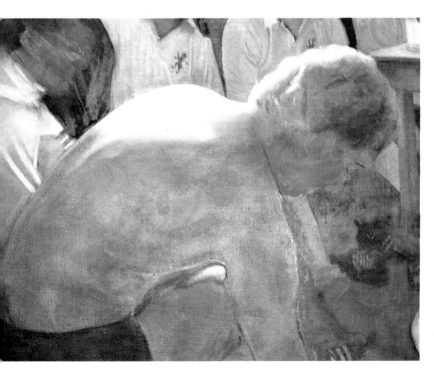

*In another rugby changing-room
sketch, effects of light and pose can
be found that you could not recreate
in a studio.*

Painting People

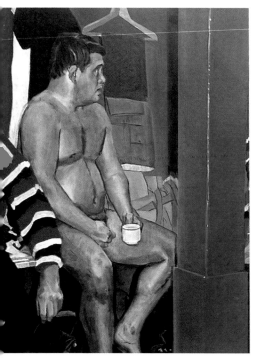

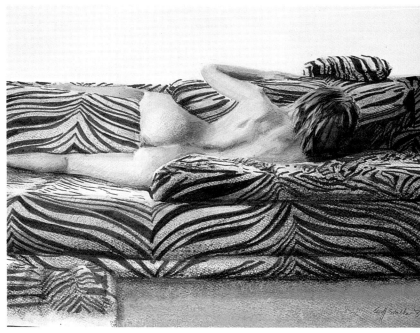

Try to paint a nude in the context a nude is found, Ingres' Turkish bath for example, or here in a rugby changing room. This painting started out as a pencil sketch; then it moved on to a study of dirty, sweaty flesh, and lots of it.

Arrange your model in animated poses, ones that would be unsuitable with a clothed figure. Note the muscular tensions in strained poses.

You can try all the experiments and adventures you wish with a life model, who is there solely for the purpose of posing for a painting.

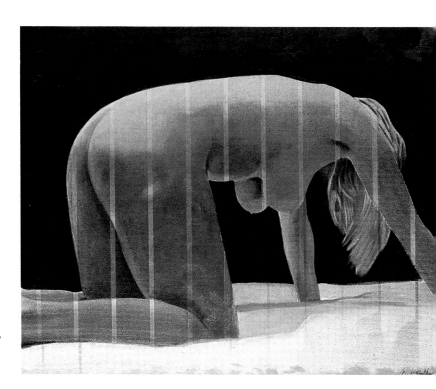

Quick oil sketches, as in this case oil on brown wrapping paper, can be made in a few minutes. Give yourself a time limit, say fifteen minutes, or restrict yourself to four colours.

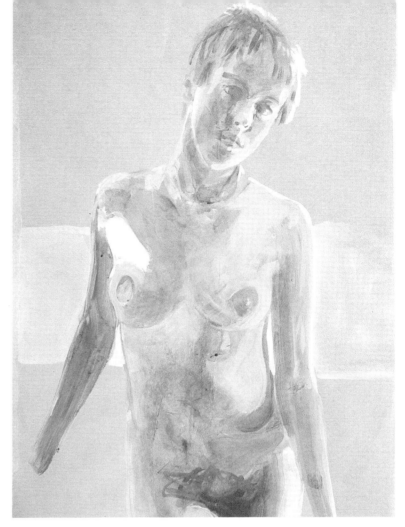

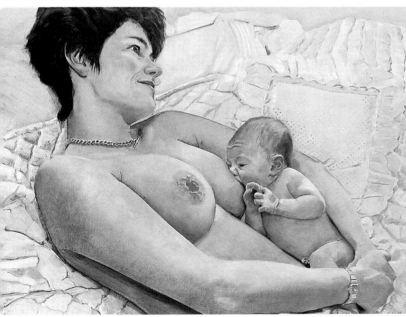

Painting a mother with a newborn baby had, by the very nature of things, to be a quick painting. I used a mixture of quick-drying gel and turpentine, and treated the painting rather like a watercolour. The hardest part was steering a course between any 'Madonna' or 'Christmas card' overtones and the raw facts of motherhood and childbirth.

PAINTING LANDSCAPES

A small intimate detail can say as much about a landscape as a vast panoramic view. In this study of a mountain stream, the little white dots of paint define the shapes of the rocks, foliage and water as well as express the atmosphere both spiritual and meteorological.

Landscape painting is very much an English art form. Although Claude and Poussin in seventeenth-century France were the first giants of European landscape painting, they used landscape only as a backdrop for their classical dramas. Similarly, Hobbemma and Ruysdael in Holland explored landscape as the scene of quiet, contemporary, almost agricultural dramas. It was Constable and Turner who explored the inherent drama of landscape itself.

Constable was one of the first artists to take his oils out into the middle of a field, plant his easel down and paint what he saw. Clouds, rainstorms, trees in sunlight, the shimmering of a tree in the wind were not just the subjects of his thousands of studies, but of his major academy painting. In England in the early 1800s landscape painting was not considered 'high art'; Constable and Turner changed all that. Although Turner painted many classical themes from Greek and Roman mythology, we admire him now for strapping himself to the mast of a ship in a sea storm and painting the fury of the sea. I particularly like his reaction to the burning of the Houses of Parliament in 1834: he did not rush to help put the fire out, he got out his paints and celebrated the event on canvas.

This acceptance of nature on her

Painting outdoors in England is a sizeable chunk of the tourist industry these days. Art magazines are full of advertisements for painting holidays and sketching weekends. The itinerant artist is as much a part of a summer beauty spot as bird song.

I was out painting recently when a couple of American tourists happened by. They took a photograph of me. I included them in my painting. Their photograph is probably called "Artist at work in Constable country". The irony of the whole scene was completed when two American Airforce jets flew less than a hundred feet over our heads.

own terms was not just painting's answer to the poems of Wordsworth and Coleridge, it was a major turning point in the history of Western European art.

What a wonderful invention the tube is. An American portrait painter John G. Rand invented the tin-tube in 1841. Lead tubes had been tried but they reacted with the pigments of the paint. In the early 1800s, artists like Turner had to make do with paint wrapped in little pigs' bladders. There is a glass cabinet at the Tate Gallery in London which displays all Turner's paraphernalia for painting: all the raw unground pigments and the various oils and mediums to mix them with.

Then along come those handy little tubes and artists like Monet, Manet, Renoir and Degas could go off on trips to the meadow, the ballet rehearsal, or the seaside, and paint to their heart's content.

Not only did the invention of the tube allow the artist to take his studio out into the fresh air, the newly invented pigments that were packed into these tubes allowed the artists to bring some fresh air into their studios.

Of all the equipment in this portable 'studio' the most important is the stool. Starve in a garret if you wish, but you should be comfortable when you work.

Stones, parsley, dead leaves, some polythene and an old mirror can give you the beginnings of an imaginary landscape.

Choosing a location with a pin for a landscape study is not without its hazards. Barbed wire and three fields of breeding bulls had to be negotiated. The site has an eerie quality, the sort of place where you might imagine a dead body to be buried.

Painting Landscapes

Exercise

To get to grips with what real landscape painting is all about, I am going to suggest two exercises:

1. Follow the example of a minor eighteenth-century English landscape painter, Alexander Cozens, who would collect a mirror, some lumps of coal, a few rocks and some small plants and shrubs and compose a small landscape on a tabletop near his studio window. The mirror would act as a lake, the plants would be set out as trees and in the background there would be 'mountains' of coal. You can play about with the positions of the various elements to make your ideal landscape. Do a painting of your little construction.

2. For the second exercise, you need to obtain an Ordnance Survey map of your area. Choose a public footpath and stick a pin in a suitable spot. Choose a direction on the throw of a dice and go out and paint what you see. Accept what you see; don't try to change anything or tidy things up.

Before going out to paint a landscape, set up your palette. Use the bottom of a plastic butter carton and put your mediums and solvents in those little marmalade and jam-jars you get from motorway service stations. Do not bother with those cheap, flimsy portable easels; nail your canvas to a tree or a fence post, where it will be much more stable.

'Winwick'
Watercolour is often regarded as the most convenient medium for painting the English landscape in the English climate. The soft muted tones of watercolour suit the misty greens and greys of the countryside. You can get these same colours with oils and a greater variety of texture and hue to boot. Oils are much more versatile and immediate.

I was asked to do a painting of Dunchurch to be used as a gift for its twin town in France 'Ferriers-en Brie'. It was painted from the comfort of a well-appointed hotel window.

Exercise

There are two more exercises I should like to suggest to you, which involve different approaches in techniques as well as different approaches to the process of looking.

1. Choose a setting with several different elements in it: trees, buildings, a couple of figures, and so on. Use a sable brush and very thin paint and draw each individual separate element. Identify each separate tree with its outline. Construct the buildings, get the perspective right. Rebuild your picture with the lines of your brush as if you were drawing a still life with pencil. Ignore the effects of light and of weather and of the fleeting moment. When you have completed your drawing in paint set about painting your scene to emphasize the separate identity of each of the elements of your picture.

2. The same scene. Instead of identifying each tree, building, figure, look for and identify each separate colour. Some ochres may be common to both the trees and the buildings, some greens may unite the trees and a distant field, some dark umbers and deep blues may link the shadows of the trees and some passing lorry. Squint your eyes and look through your eyelashes, it will help you to forget that the tree is a tree, the house is a house, it will help you rid the setting of both outline and label. Just paint the colours and the tones as you see them.

Whichever exercise you do first, you will find that each approach informs the other.

'Yelvertoft Ditch', 'Brooks Ditch'
These two ditches are in reality about a yard apart. However, the emphasis in the first is on shape and form, the hardness of the twigs and stodginess of the mud. In the second, I pay more attention to the effects of light and colour. Shape and form are incidental to the visual play between the twigs, the reflection of the twigs on the surface of the water, and the texture of the mud at the bottom of the ditch.

'Massey's second ditch'
This painting looks down below the
level of the horizon. Shape, form,
texture, weight are the elements to get
across.

So far, I have only talked about pair
ing landscapes out of doors. 'Stud
landscapes' are just as valid and wor
while, but you must do your resear
in the form of lots of sketches, phot
graphs and drawings. In the studi
you can bring consideration, care ai
detail to your landscape. Painti
landscapes should not be restrict
to those artists who can stand t
cold.

The most important aspect of a
landscape or outdoor study is t
eye-line or horizon. Like the key
music, it dictates the weight of a p
ture. The same scene with two pai
ings, one with its horizon at the top
the picture and the other with
horizon at the bottom, will be tota
different, not just in content but
character.

'Looking for dead bodies'
Looking up into the trees with the
horizon at the bottom of the picture,
the patterns of the branches and the
interplay of colours as the sky is seen
through the foliage, take over the
painting.

Exercise

Find a suitably idyllic spot in the middle of nowhere and make three more studies. The first should be with the horizon below the bottom of your picture. Look up through trees at clouds, perhaps; include the edge of a building or telegraph pole.

The second study should be made with the horizon in the middle of your picture. The third study should be looking downwards, some tree roots, the reflection of the sky in the dirty water of a ditch, the horizon way above the top of your picture.

You will find that the first study will be all pattern and light as you pick out the delicate tracery of the twigs and branches against the sky. Your brushwork will emphasize the colour of the foliage with light shining on it as well as through it.

The second study will be all depth and space where you pick out the linear perspective of trees and buildings receding into the distance and the aerial perspective as the colours become more muted the further away they are.

The third study will be all texture and shape as you note the differing qualities of the foliage, the soil, the tree roots.

You may feel that you wish to challenge my preconceptions in your painting as Gainsborough challenged Reynolds.

Rachel with Cows
The horizon need not necessarily be painted in for it to have an influence on your picture. The eye-line, slightly below the backs of the cows, combined with the flat lawn, imply that the painter or viewer is sitting down. This is a factor in maintaining the interplay between the comic and the menacing.

The horizon does not have to be perfectly level.

53

Landscape – Step-by-Step

There is a gated road near where I live which the farmer protects from ramblers, joggers and busy-bodies by keeping rutting bulls in the fields through which the path wanders. About three miles down this rarely trodden path, there is a copse and a stagnant duck pond. There are no ducks, in fact there is very little wild-life; no bird song, no rabbits, just the rustle of rats and the occasional bark of a dog fox. It is a remote and secret place.

This is where I decided to make my painting. I did not make any pre-paratory sketches, and I decided to be there from five o'clock to seven o'clock every night for five days. A beech tree acted as an adequate easel, and I painted on a 36in × 54in grey-primed board.

Step 1   *I made some preparatory scribbles with oil pastel sticks and coloured pencils, just to help me get my bearings in a complex scene.*

Light filtered through the trees and bounced off the pond in patterns of dots. This was balanced by the leaf mould and twigs on the copse floor. Half a dozen tree trunks provided the only elements of shape and solidity.

Step 2   *A thin sable brush loaded with Zinc White was used to map out the patterns of dots that make up the sky and branches. A Pale Green is used similarly to pick out the fields and the fence.*

Step 3   *In bright sunlit scenes, the first things to take account of are shadows. In this dark, melancholy spot I had to establish the light from the sky and its reflection in the pond, and also the light from the field beyond the fence.*

Step 4 *This green and yellow reflected light seems brighter than the direct light of the sky (one of the little paradoxes of colour). I put a dark outline round the green and started establishing some tonal values.*

Step 5 *At this stage, I needed to darken the rest of the picture to get somewhere closer to the mood of the scene. More than this, however, I had to get rid of the pristine grey primer. It is too clean and neat. We needed some paint and some brush marks here. So I took whatever dark paints were left on my palette and mixed them with quick-drying medium.*

Step 6 *The sky seen through the trees at the top left is a complex image. It is always shifting in the slight breeze. The main trunks and branches of the trees give a structure and a rhythm. Squinting through the eyelashes helps to simplify things.*

Step 7 The black lines of the twigs and branches were painted with a thin sable brush and a mixture of Ultramarine, Indigo, Olive Green, Burnt Sienna, and some Blue Mauve. The paint is diluted with turpentine to help it flow off the brush like watercolour.

Step 8 The white bits of the sky were painted with a medium sable brush in a stabbing motion. The white paint was mixed with quick-drying 'wingel'. I needed it to dry overnight because there would be constant repainting of this section; first the dark linear bits, then the white blobs.

Step 10 The process of painting is a means of making one look closer, more intently. The tree trunks are difficult, not because they are hard to paint, but because they are hard to see, to perceive.

Step 9 I could possibly have got away with a quick 'impression' of this section, but I needed to be as accurate as possible, partly because the rhythms of the negative and positive shapes are botanically different from tree to tree, bush to bush, but more because it may be these quirky shapes that give the scene its character. I don't know. I have just got to keep painting to find out.

56

Step 11 *The two tree trunks on the right are in an awkward place from a compositional point of view, but they are there; I have to accept them; I have started so I will finish.*

The leaves, twigs and debris on the floor were enormously difficult to paint. I stuck four garden canes at 2ft (60cm) apart to help me see what was there. Having done that, I lost my nerve and did some easy painting in a swathe across the middle of the picture.

Step 12 *When I finally plucked up the courage to paint the ground I did so in white, to establish the tonal values. I used a thin, long-bristled sign-writer's brush and a little liquin as a binding agent.*

Step 13 *The marks that I made and the actions I made in painting them suggest Chinese or Japanese writing, perhaps Egyptian hieroglyphs. Perhaps there is some deep, philosophical truth about the origin of writing and language that my mind cannot quite grasp. It occurs to me, however, that just as gesture and inflexion are expressed in Japanese characters, so the marks that I am making have their own meaning, a visual meaning.*

Step 15 *Here I hit a major irony. This half acre of botanical detritus is abstract in every sense of the word.*

Step 14 *Having established the tonal values in sketch form, I set about some serious painting. I used a full palette here. I was not trying to create a photographic illusion of every twig and dead leaf, but trying to use paint to account for the visual effect of each leaf and twig.*

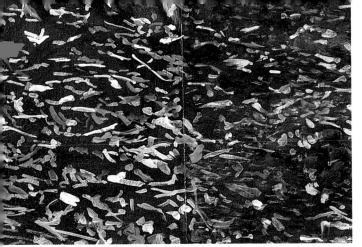

Step 16 *The elements that make it up have no name. When does a leaf become leaf mould? When does a twig become compost? And when does compost become soil? What sort of visual identity does it have when a breeze or a frost can come along and totally change it?*

Step 17 *I made a stab at painting it, section by section. I did not get the colours right or the trees right, but these can be modified later with some transparent glazes and opaque highlights.*

In the meantime, I returned to the fence and the field for some easy looking.

Step 18 *I established the reflections in the pond and the picture began to have a character.*

Step 19 *There is a sort of bond between the picture and the scene where I know what is right and what is wrong. The tree and sky began to take shape, but not colour.*

Step 20 *The area beyond the pond on the left and the trees in the background on the right, I just could not see, let alone paint.*

Step 21 *I returned to the floor and modified some shapes with liquin-based glazes; this inevitably is a little lumpy.*

Step 22 Something clicks. My perception of the floor is not a purely visual one: apart from the smell and the sounds, there is an apparent tactile quality, a sense of what it must feel like to touch. Whilst the gobs of paint glaze do not feel like twigs and leaves, they do at least break up the flatness of the painting's surface.

I was tempted to leave the garden canes where they were and paint them into the picture; they had now become part of the scene. But I took them away and, having done this, I could not put them back. Their purpose changed from being an aid to my drawing to being a bit of painterly perversity.

I put the canes back, however, but did not paint them.

SCALE

Have you ever gone to the cinema to watch a really good film, been totally bowled over by it, then twenty-five years later seen the same film on television and been really disappointed?

Or have you bought an art book on a particular artist and been really impressed with the 6 × 4in (15 × 10cm) reproduction of a painting, made the pilgrimage to the appropriate gallery and been crestfallen when the same 6 × 4ft (180 × 120cm) painting is not the masterpiece you thought?

SIZE IS IMPORTANT

At the cinema, what is happening on the screen almost fills your field of vision and, in the darkened theatre, your suspension of disbelief is total because there is nothing to distract you. At home, watching TV, the screen takes up not more than 10 per cent of your field of vision: you can see the fireplace, the newspaper on the coffee table and even through the window.

A small reproduction in a book on your lap has a jewel-like quality. It is at arm's length; it has flattened out all the little bumps and brushmarks, it has eliminated all the quirks of light and reflection. But more than this,

> **Exercise**
>
> Make the biggest canvas that you can manage (but small enough to get through the door of the studio!) Choose the smallest, most precious theme to paint, a cameo ring on a finger, a coin, a dried-up leaf. Put some heavy-metal rock music or some grand opera on the radio and splash about with controlled abandon.

This large profile of a girl's head is 6 × 4ft (180 × 120cm) with a raw hessian canvas, lightly primed. The subject was a seventeen-year-old American girl who lived with my family for a while. She was extremely lovely and I had painted her a couple of times; then I wanted to do a profile of her as an emblem rather than a portrait. The Queen's head on a coin or stamp is in the same sense an emblem rather than a portrait.

I deliberately got myself into a mess using all sorts of paint from emulsion, household gloss, even shoe-colour restorer. The physicality of the painting was as important as Jessica's physical presence. I then set about unifying the picture with dashes of oil paint, using a range of flat household brushes. For the solid, bony highlights of the face I used colours close in tone and hue. The application of paint involved moving my shoulders, back and elbows rather than my finger tips, and standing on a chair rather than sitting on it.

the reproduction can be taken in all at one glance, at a convenient focal length and without moving the eye-balls.

Standing in front of a great Rubens, it occupies your full field of vision; you have to move around to take it all in. You go up to it to examine a small detail, your head moves, your whole body moves in response to the physicality of this large picture.

There is in the National Gallery, London, a small room given over to small religious icons from the fifteenth century. Those tiny precious objects with their gold leaf and their lapis lazuli blues and their minute details of Madonna's fingernails and lace bodices, painted with a brush made from two hairs, guide the spectator closer and closer to them. This room is the quietest and stillest in the whole gallery.

The scale factor is more important in oil painting than in any other medium because the size of a painting affects the technique.

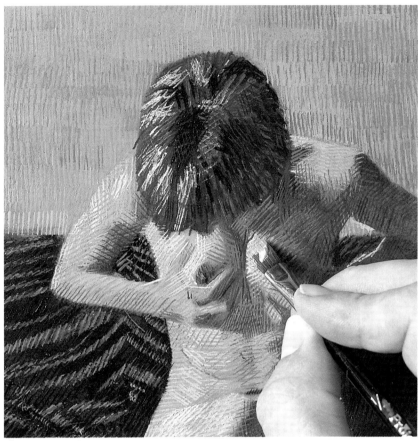

Exercise

Take as your theme or subject a large landscape, a crowd scene, the high point in a favourite drama. Get the smallest canvas from your art shop or a little off-cut of hardboard. Sit down by a table top, get comfortable and execute this grand masterpiece on a tiny scale. Use sable watercolour brushes and turpentine as a medium. Perhaps you might put Beethoven's last quartets on the record player.

This painting of a nude is only 13 × 9in (33 × 23cm), a panel of hardboard so small that it does not require a supporting frame. I painted it on my lap using a flat 1cm sable brush. No binding agent or turpentine was used, only a rag to wipe off the excess paint from my brush, and moving only the knuckles of three fingers. The heel of the hand has to rest on something solid as the dashes of colour are laid down. The figure was moving slightly but not enough to make movement a major element in the composition.

It is an intimate picture in composition as well as subject matter. The colours, clear and individual marks have a jewel like quality, not because they are taken 'straight from the tube' but because I mix complementaries at the same time.

BRUSHES

To all intents and purposes, a brush is anything that will allow you to take paint from a tube or palette and transfer it satisfactorily on to your canvas. As well as the most expensive sable brushes, I include within this definition, household and industrial brushes, rollers, bits of sponge and rags, fingers and hands, palette knives and spatulas.

The modern brush with its flattened metal ferrule or collar was only developed in the nineteenth century. This led to the flat, wedge-shaped brushes that were so influential in the development of the impressionists' technique. They could load their brushes heavily and still produce delicate strokes and touches. Artists of the Italian Renaissance had to make do with a few hairs wrapped round a stick and tied with a wire.

Bristle brushes are cheap and are good for rough preparatory work and for soft gradations of tone and colour. They do lose the occasional hair though.

For delicate detail and line work, use a sable brush. They are quite expensive but if you look after them well, they will last a long time. They have a certain spring in their body, which is invaluable with oil. After use, you should clean them thoroughly, giving them a final rinse with soapy water. Squeeze the fibres with thumb and forefinger so that it dries in shape.

There's a whole range of new artificial fibres used in brushes. Mostly, they come under the generic title of nylon, but they vary enormously in flexibility, fibre thickness and body. I can only suggest that you buy one of each and experiment.

The old palette knife seems to have gone out of fashion since the 'kitchen-sink realists' of the 1950s and 1960s. The palette knife is still of value for little touches of pure colour and for building up texture and body in your

A range of modern brushes with a metal ferrule to bind the bristles to the wooden handle.

For soft delicate half tones and little blushes of colour you can't beat an old worn out brush. Just put a little stain of colour on the fibres and gently touch up your pictures as if you were applying make-up.

painting. A spatula works in the same way as a palette knife for broad, painterly gestures and flourishes. Plastic credit cards are perfect for broad areas of colour and also for delicate straight lines.

Try to get hold of one of those signwriters' brushes with the very long bristles. Not only are they excellent for accurate line work, but you can

Household sweeping brushes and wallpaper brushes can be used for stippling soft gradations of colour and tone.

You can create a nice contour or outline with a flat brush by using it at an angle and forcing the paint to the edge of the brush. With thick paint or an impasto binding medium you can sculpt the paint into quite heavy ridges.

get some wonderful painterly effects by loading with two or three colours at once and rolling the brush across your canvas.

Cotton buds and discarded make-up can be used for direct applications of paint as well as subtle modifications of colour. It is amazing how many women who can transform themselves with make-up say they cannot paint.

Often, the composition of a painting dictates the technique. In this portrait of an ex-England rugby player, I wanted the white of the shirts to play an important part in the composition, with the little red lions and the red rose making a nice link.

I started out painting the shirts, using a 1in (2.5cm) household brush and raw, undiluted Zinc White. I was impatient and I could not wait for the slow-drying white paint to dry, so I used a household sponge paint roller to take off the excess paint. I then used lumps of the sponge roller to rub in the underpaint for the figure (a mixture of Raw Sienna, Leaf Green and a touch of Alizarin Crimson). It was one of those good days when you realize you have worked well only at the very end. I let the paint dry before the next stage. The shadows in the white shirts were quite easy, but the soft modulations of the folds were more of a problem. Small details like the lions and the rose were painted in with a brush, then sponged away to maintain a consistency of surface texture. A similar method was used for the background shadows. For the flesh tones in the figure, I laid out five or six different light tones and a similar number of dark tones for the shadows.

I spread each colour out in a thin film over the palette with my thumb so that I did not take up too much paint with my sponge. I tested each spongeful on an old white board. For detailed work I made a few sponge brushes by taping little bits of ¼in (7mm) thick sponge to an old brush. I wiped away any small mistakes with cotton buds.

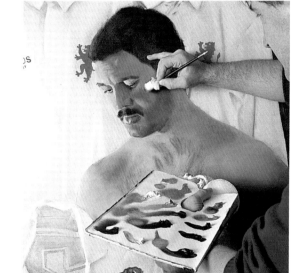

Brushes

You can use rags and sponges for finished work also. Using some strong masking tape you could make little 'brushes' by fixing your rag or sponge to the back of an old brush or pencil and using them in a dabbing motion. Judicious use of masking tape can achieve remarkable effects of subtlety and delicacy.

To build up texture in my painting, I use a palette knife or a 1in (2.5cm) household brush when I do my under-painting or fill in broad areas of colour.

However, if I want my final work to have a smooth even surface, my preparatory work is done with a rag or sponge. Corduroy, towelling, or old curtains are ideal because they will not deposit little bits of fibre or fluff on to your work. There are many different kinds of sponge: scouring pads, bathroom sponges, upholstery sponges, even natural sponge. They have different elasticity and textures; again, buy one of each and experiment.

A mixture of sponge work on the face and brush work for the hair and a rag for the background frosted window.

Make sure that you are in full command of the purity and tone of your colour. The flat pancake of colour on your palette will look very different when converted to the fine mists and speckles of the stippled paint on your canvas.

Flicking the loaded bristles of colour with the finger or dabbing the fibre ends directly on to the canvas will give you slightly different effects. Again experiment, experiment, ex-periment. With oil paint, all mistakes can be undone.

Of course, the oldest brush in the world is the human finger. It was used to paint the first cave paintings; Rembrandt's masterpieces are covered with his thumb prints. We all did finger-painting at junior school but in even the most sophisticated work, you can use your finger to soften a line or tone down a highlight, or blend a couple of colours.

'Massey's ditch'
The edge of this little woodland stream gave me the opportunity of using several different types of brush in the same picture.

I wanted the structure of the paint and the brushstrokes that I made to create not just an illusion of the scene but a series of metaphors for it as well. In other words for the water at the bottom of the picture, I wanted to put down the paint in great gobs of clear, translucent colour.

For the wet grass, I used long flowing strokes with a long thin sign-writer's brush. For the dried twigs and the trunks of the saplings, I used hard, straight movements with a short, flat brush and thick, dry paint. I had drawn a lot of the details in pencil so there was nearly as much trial as error. The deep shadows were a mixture of Prussian Blue, Indigo and Burnt Sienna, rubbed into the canvas with an old square brush.

There were lots of very difficult sections, but there were some fun, easy bits as well. The mud at the water's edge was just a load of scrapings from yesterday's palette, mixed up with some liquin and sludged into the canvas. For the ripples in the water, I rolled a round, hog's hair brush in some linseed oil, picked up the odd dot of colour, two or three at a time, and rolled the lot into approximately the right area.

In the middle of the work, I was in a mess. A rescue act was performed by redrawing with thin black paint, re-establishing the shapes and outlining some of the more difficult details. Then it was back to experiment, mud and mess.

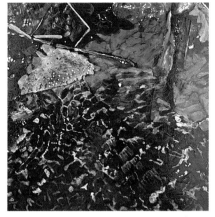

A final stage of re-establishing the shadows and some redrawing of the shapes was rounded off by picking out the highlights and reflections. A thin brush, a load of Titanium White, a dab here, a dab there, lots of mistakes, but none that can be detected by anyone but me. A month later, I return to the picture to put a few things right and a full stop in the bottom right-hand corner.

Line

The use of line in oil painting is a very complex subject in art history, and an even more complex one in the practical business of applying oil paint to a picture. We carry with us a baggage of visual conventions framed by watching cartoons on television, which are black outlines filled with flat colour, or through reading comics and strip cartoons, which are pure black line. In our art lessons at school we are taught to draw out our ideas in pencil first before we proceed to paint our picture. The chances are that if you were a good art student you were taught not just to draw and paint using line but to see, think and perceive in linear terms.

Line can be used not just to define the contour of a shape but also to express the essential structure of a shape, both two dimensionally on the canvas and three dimensionally in the implied illusion of the image created.

The expressive quality of the lines you paint is often dictated by the sort of brush you use and the nature of your paint.

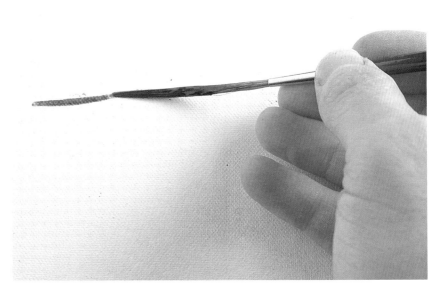

A long-bristled sign-writer's brush with very thin paint will give you a crisp precise line. You can paint long straight lines and gently rounded curves.

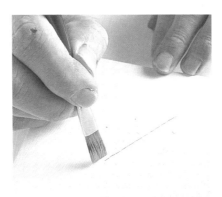

A flat, sable brush with undiluted paint is ideal for creating thin straight lines.

Exercise 1

Choose as your subject something that is essentially linear in character; a sod of grass; the hands of an old woman knitting; a knot of old rope. Without picking out the outline of any of the shapes try and use the rhythms of your brush to express your subject.

Exercise 2

Try and do the same thing as described in Exercise 1, without any preparatory drawing.

You can also use it to create a 'negative' line, that is, leaving the line blank and painting everything around it.

Exercise 3

Same subject matter as above, but this time paint only those points where one line goes behind another. Omit or sketch in lightly all other lines; just focus your attention on the cross-overs or junctions.

The line of this old lady's mouth is crucial to the character of the portrait. An underpaint of bluish-brown was painted and the lips filled in with ochres, pinks and magenta up to the line of the mouth. This created a negative line, which is more accurate and expressive than a thin black painted line would have been.

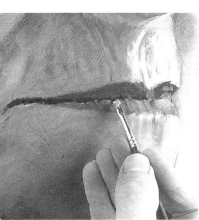

I want to pick out four different lines in this detail. There is the wet hair of the little girl, which is a round solid shape. This can be expressed by using a heavily loaded brush of white and Naples Yellow and building up the linear brush strokes on an area of dark underpainting.

By contrast, a worn-out old brush with the slightest stain of Burnt Sienna paint when applied in a delicate manner can express not just the shape of the man's legs but also their characteristic hairiness.

The flesh of the old man in the background is wrinkly and sits loosely on the bone structure of the arm and rib-cage. The different kinds of line within the structure are best expressed by painting in the highlights with a small, hard brush and very dry paint. I used as a base some Flake White which had been left on the palette for a few days.

The line of the edge of the shorts is not an important one to the composition. Nor does this line indicate a change of shape or direction. So I do my best to

play down this line. I have also eliminated the red and white striped pattern of the shorts.

Very expressive lines can be created by using the back of your brush and scraping away fresh paint to reveal the blank canvas or underpainting beneath. Rembrandt used this technique to great effect.

The lines of the texture of this wet bark are created by mixing dark, greenish-brown paint with a lot of liquin or linseed oil, and using a broad brush, pressing hard on the canvas. The edges of the brushstrokes form ridges of dark colour while the middle of the brushstroke is thin and semi-transparent.

TEXTURE

The nature of the surface of a painting is a vital part of its aesthetic quality. One of the limitations of watercolour is that the surface quality is controlled by the paper you are using. With oil paint, the variety of textures and effects that you can achieve is endless.

I have already touched on the quality of canvas you work on and the variety of grounds you can use in the preparation of a working canvas.

Using rough hessian with only a couple of coats of primer immediately makes one aware of the feel of the surface. After laying on all the underpaint, one can modulate all the tones and colours by lightly touching the ridges of the canvas with tiny lumps or dots of colour.

Using the same hessian but with several layers of primer and a deal of sandpapering, there are still ridges and furrows to work with but they are essentially smooth and rounded off. With this surface, one can fill in the furrows or valleys with thin translucent paint, diluted with linseed oil and turpentine.

Sometimes the texture just builds up as a result of working and re-

'Blue Ditch'
In this picture, the paint is sculpted in the same shapes as the flow of the colour. The strong brush lines of the twigs, the swirls of the stream and the rounded form of the pebbles are laid down with heavy impasto.

'And all your raging glory'
In the sky of this painting, however, the trickles of paint and the flow of colour are not always consistent. This helps to strike a discordant note.

Experiment

Sometimes you need a head start to break up the smooth nature of your canvas and make you aware of the surface quality of a painting. The texture of an old rejected painting is always a good start, or you could stick objects to your canvas, drill holes in your hardboard, or use one of the proprietary brands of wall texturizer. If you are doing a woodland scene, stick dried leaves on to your canvas before you prime it. If you are painting clothes, stick down bits of cloth, or if you are doing a nude, take great handfuls of primer and caress it into the shape of your figure; if you can afford it, you could continue the painting with sensuous handfuls of paint and linseed oil.

working an image. Occasionally you are tempted to sand down and start again; at other times the build-up of paint acts as a history of the working of the painting.

By dragging a brush loaded with undiluted paint across the surface of a texture or rough canvas the paint will be deposited on the 'peaks'. These little spots of colour can be used to emphasize the texture or blend two colours together. Sometimes you can give a colour a bit of a boost by 'hiding' the occasional touch of the colour's opposite, or complementary.

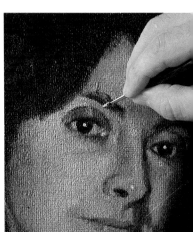

'Rachel and Allison'
An alternative technique for mixing colours on a textured
surface is to float some paint diluted with thin oil or
turpentine into the valleys of the canvas weave. The peaks
of the texture will maintain their original colour and the
valleys will fill up with colour.

A heavy impasto painting can
produce both texture and pattern in
the same brush work. Often you can
create a harmony of texture and
pattern; at other times you can get the
pattern to work contrary to the rhythm
and texture of your paint.

The corduroy which was used as a
'canvas' for this painting not only gave
me a chance to play with pairs or
groups of colours on the surface, but
the texture of the corduroy gives the
whole picture a rhythm, a feel. I could
still get involved with small intimate
details, but the surface texture and
direction of the stripes of the corduroy
gave a consistency to the brush work.

The lace blouse on this lady could
have been rendered with fine detail on
a smooth surface. However the tactile
quality of the lace and the flesh seen
through the holes, made it a
wonderful material to paint. Building
up the paint in lumps, layer upon
layer, allowed me to create ridges of
hard white paint which catch the light
in the same way as the ridges of the
lace do.

MASKING TECHNIQUES

I have a whole range of masking tapes and masking films. I do not use them just to help me paint straight lines and hard edges: sometimes I like to mask off a whole area of a picture so that I may concentrate on a particularly difficult detail.

Proprietary brands of masking tape and sticky tape, and plastic electrical tape are very good if your paint is dry and you need a precise hard edge. Typist's correction tape is made of thin paper and has a light adhesive quality. It will not tear your painting from its canvas but you have to handle it carefully or it may move when you are using it. Of a similar quality are those peel on, peel off note pads. Overlapping several together you can create curves and rounded forms. If you need to make a stencil to repeat a pattern shape, they are just the thing.

Fablon or adhesive kitchen film will allow you to cut out intricate shapes with a scalpel. If you stick the whole film onto your canvas, and you are careful not to cut your canvas with the scalpel, you can keep peeling away the adhesive film as you add each new colour. This technique usually leads to a painting with crisp, hard edges and areas of flat colour. This is a good discipline to use if you are thinking of making a silk-screen or lino-block print from your painting when you have finished.

I had a particular problem with this painting of two sisters. I had the broad curve of the table top as a major element in the composition and I wanted to set it off against the grid of the window frames. I had previously drawn in the frames with a coloured pencil and ruler and painted them freehand, but it was a long laborious process, and it looked it when I had finished. I wanted the straight lines to be absolutely, mathematically straight and the edges to be

nice and crisp. So, with a rag, I wiped off the frames that I had painted and proceeded to mask off the frames with masking tape. However, the paint was not yet dry and the masking tape would not stick to the wet oil paint. So I had to wipe the paint over again with a sponge soaked in turpentine and leave overnight to dry.

The next day, I used 2in (5cm) tape with a stronger adhesive quality. This partially did the trick. Taking care to brush away from the tape with a lightly loaded brush, I achieved the desired effect. However, when I pulled the tape away, I removed part of the mouth of the girl in the white blouse, because the tape I had used was too sticky, and had brought away with it some colours that were touch dry, but obviously not dry enough.

Masking tapes usually go hand in hand with sponging, stippling or spray techniques, as I have described earlier. In order to achieve soft edges with these methods, you can stick various thicknesses of cardboard to your canvas. A basic rule of thumb is that the thicker the card, the softer the edge you will achieve.

Two minor reservations I have about any of the masking methods are that firstly, it puts me one step away from direct contact with the canvas and, secondly, it exerts too much of an influence on the nature of the marks I make, the brushwork.

Although oil paint is not as versatile as acrylics for spray gun techniques, it is wonderful for stippling. You can buy proper stippling brushes if you like but real skill in any stipple work lies in masking out, and not in how well you can flick the fibres of your brush. Toothbrushes, shoe-polish brushes, scrubbing brushes and nail brushes are as good as anything you can buy in any art shop. Spread your paint out evenly on your palette before you dip your brush in. An errant lump of paint can ruin your picture.

Crocodile ditch *I was having problems with the reflected sky in this picture. The logs, the lily pads and the water were perfectly still. The clouds, however, were moving quite quickly. As well as adapting to the changes in light, I had to express the movement of the clouds. This entailed some animated gestures of the brush. To protect the rest of my picture I masked off everything but the reflected clouds and set to work with wild abandon.*

71

TAKING PAINT AWAY

If you were doing a pencil drawing, you would not think of starting without an eraser handy. When you are using oil, you should always have a clean lint-free rag available or an old towel or curtain cut up into handy 1ft (30cm) squares. The rag can be used not just to take away or rub out any mistakes, useful though that is, but as part of a positive technique.

If the overall colour balance of your painting is perhaps a little too yellow, wait until your picture is dry, then give a thin wash of translucent purple with a liquin or linseed-oil base. Use the rag to take the bulk of the paint away, to give you an extremely thin layer of paint, which will subtly modify the yellowness.

Soft gradations of tone and colour can be achieved by using a sponge to take away parts of a layer of paint so that more of a particular area of under-paint shines through the surface layer. This is particularly useful in portrait painting.

More linear effects can be achieved by using a clean, dry brush with just a hint of turpentine on it. The less tur-

You can use an old rag or an old brush to rub away undried paint or to create negative lines and shapes.

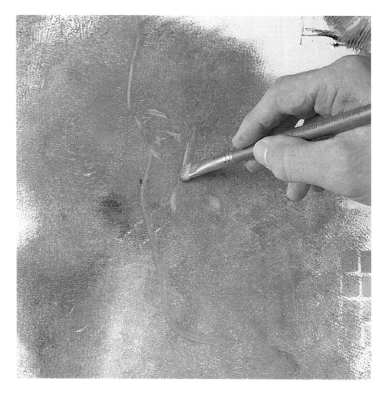

Exercise 1

Set up a still life or figure study with a lighted candle or lampshade, something with dramatic lighting and sharp contrasts. Using a white-primed canvas, cover with a layer of Pure Black paint straight from the tube. Use the tip of your brush handle to draw through the black paint to reveal a white line. Build up your picture by sponging and brushing away the black paint to reveal the various tones of white and grey. How close you get to the real thing is up to you; you may wish to let it dry before touching up details.

You can use sandpaper not just to pare down dried lumps of paint and prepare a flat surface, but also to create subtle gradations of colour as you cut through one layer of paint to the one below.

The sky in the background of the old man's portrait was a bad mistake. I put down a layer of paint that was far too strong in hue. It was nearly the right tone so I sanded the occasional lump of paint down and applied another layer of blue with a hint of Cadmium Orange in it. I also added some Zinc White. Using a rag, I then took away this second layer of paint until a combination of the first layer and the second layer gave me the hue and the tone I wanted.

pentine you have on your brush, the softer the line will be. By using more you will achieve a clean, negative line.

Dean Richards detail
For sharper negative lines, use the tip of a brush handle, either for a precise rendering of shapes and lines, or for more subtle effects. Here, the cheek bones, the cleft in the upper lip and the odd touch of scar tissue are picked out with the tip of a brush handle.

Exercise 2

Make the same study as in Exercise 1, but this time lay down an area of yellow over your white-primed canvas. Draw and sponge away as above, then let it dry for a few days. When the yellow is dry, put on a layer of red and repeat the sponging-away process with green, blue, purple, and so on. A variation of this is to mix the same reds, yellows, blues as the colour-printing industry does.

THE PICTURE PLANE

The picture plane is that imaginary sheet of glass which the viewer perceives as the front of the painting. The artist can place the viewer in relation to the figures or objects in his picture.

There is a wonderful 'Pieta' by Bellini in the Brera, Milan, which brings the left hand of the dead Christ through to the viewer's side of the picture plane, thus establishing the three figures as within reach, touchable. It is one of the most powerful paintings in art history.

The device of placing the edge of the table at the bottom of the picture, together with the exaggerated perspective of lines on the top of the table take the viewer right inside the rugby changing room. I wanted to screw real metal studs into the soles of the boots that Charlie Neale is holding, but I think I ran out of courage.

Titian and Rembrandt both played games with the viewer by bringing the elbows of their sitters through the picture plane of their portraits.

By the device of painting in a couple of droplets of water from the bucket or the little girl's leg, I can create a momentary illusion that the droplets are on the canvas itself. This establishes to the nearest inch where the picture plane is. On a multiple canvas like this, it is a very important element.

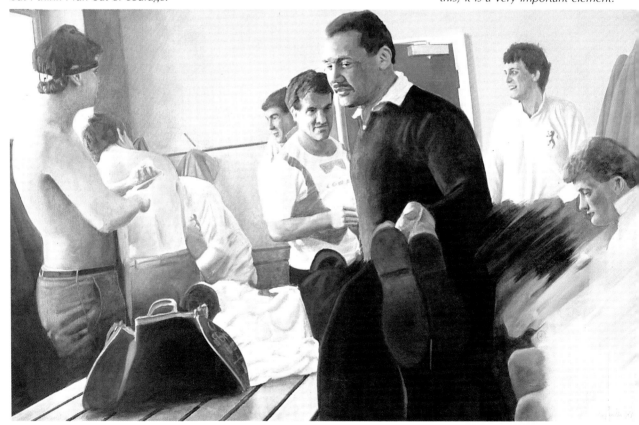

PLANNING A PAINTING

Only the very worst paintings are planned or designed. However, there are some skills of preparation that are vital to your work.

You may have produced a drawing or group of sketches that you think may be developed into a good painting. How do you transfer the drawing on to canvas?

You can trace it, like you used to do in school. Copy the basic lines and structure of your sketch, cover the back of the tracing paper with soft pencil and draw through your copy on to your canvas.

Pouncing, an old trick used in Renaissance times, particularly on frescoes, was to put pinholes along the main lines of your drawing, tape the drawing to the canvas and rub charcoal or powder paint through the pinholes on to the canvas. Take away your sketch, join up the dots as if it were a children's puzzle. This method is not of much value to an oil painter since it is cumbersome and can be messy.

Much better than both tracing and pouncing is to use typist's carbon paper. You can even get this in several colours and can produce an exciting linear image.

If you are prepared to sacrifice your sketch, cut it out section by section or colour by colour and brush in the base colour of your painting with a dry brush or sponge.

If you need to enlarge or reduce your image, there are several ways of

An epidiascope being used with photographic prints or drawings.

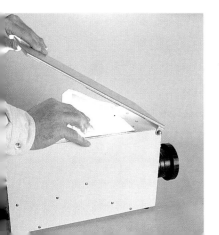

A slide projector being used with transparencies.

'squaring-up'. Draw the same rigid geometric pattern on both your sketch and your canvas. A simple grid or Union Jack will suffice as long as all the ratios and proportions are the same. Square by square, triangle by triangle, copy your sketch on to your canvas.

Use an epidiascope. This is a contraption of mirrors and lights. Place your sketch on to the glass plate and project the image on to your canvas. You can do the same for collages and magazine photos. This is only useful when working from small sketches as the largest epidiascope has only an 8 × 6in (20 × 15cm) screen.

Use a slide projector. Make a photographic slide and project the image on to your canvas. As with the epidiascope, your room needs to be dark so you can see the projected image. Unless you particularly want a distorted image, you should make sure that you project at right angles to the plane of your canvas.

An unlikely aid is a camera obscura which was used widely in the seventeenth and eighteenth centuries. Basically it is a hole in the wall with a lens. Whatever is on one side of the wall, a room or a landscape, will project itself upside-down on a canvas placed at the appropriate focal length.

It was very useful to Vermeer, we are told.

Laying a magazine photograph face down on a canvas and lightly sponging with acetone will transfer the image on to the canvas. The image will be in full colour but back to front. A word of warning, however: acetone is a dangerous chemical; it is highly inflammable and toxic. It can cause headaches and vomiting, so it may not be the method for you.

You can always transfer your sketches free-hand. What you may lose in accuracy, you may gain in freshness and spontaneity.

If you are changing the scale of whatever sketch or preparatory work, remember that a small intimate watercolour may not make the same impact as a large, grandiose oil painting.

Care must also be taken when bringing together several images or ideas. The collected elements of such a painting must share the same light source. It would be somewhat incongruous to put groups of figures, drawn and painted indoors by lamplight from the centre left, into a landscape lit by the sun in the top right of your painting.

In this large family group, however, I break my own rules. The single study of the old man and the couple below him have differing light sources from the rest of the picture. This was partly deliberate because they were painted at different times and under different conditions, but also I am allowed to be contrary if I want.

USING A CAMERA

Cheating is an important aspect of the creative process. If you can find a new and innovative way of taking a short cut, the chances are that you will have your niche in the history of Western European painting.

The first artist to use a ruler to draw a straight line was called a cheat. Ever since the camera was invented in the nineteenth century, artists who have used photographs for inspiration have been looked on with some suspicion.

Degas used a camera in his ballet and horse racing series; however he did so secretly. Vermeer, of Delft, cheated when he used a camera obscura, which was a seventeenth-century version of a slide projector. David Hockney and Francis Bacon both use photographs as their source material.

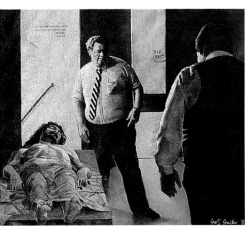

I saw in a magazine a photograph of the first man to be executed by lethal injection. The room looked mundane, but sordid, with its chalked instructions on the walls. One of the prison officers was the spitting image of an uncle of mine who was also a prison officer at the time. The dead figure was placed in such a way as to remind me of a dead Christ that Mantegna painted.

I combined the two images and incorporated my uncle in this small intimate study.

A photograph has totally different aesthetic values from a painting. For a start, it comes to us via one lens, whereas a painting has evolved through the stereoscopic medium of two human eyes. The production of a transparency or a print is essentially a mechanical one, whereas an oil painting is the product of many hand-crafts.

There are several large and successful schools of modern painting whose works have a direct relationship to photography.

The photo-realists in the USA and the super-realists in England explore areas of subject matter that would be impossible without the photographic process. The paintings of Chuck Close often incorporate the very narrow focal length of a photo. He defines space and picture depth by contrasting blurred images with high focal detail. The brush work or any sign of the hand-crafted image is eliminated by using a spray-gun.

Oil paint can be used successfully with spray techniques but you need to get the viscosity of your paint absolutely right. Thin your paint with too much spirit and the colour will only register very faintly. If your paint is too thick, it will either spot or blotch unevenly. It could even clog up your spray-gun. Acrylics lend themselves more readily to spray-gun work.

A photograph can be used to cut out the drudgery of mapping out a painting and release you from the tyranny of the drawn line. Too much time spent at the drawing stage of a painting can suck out all your spontaneity and enthusiasm. Painting should not be a matter of filling in the spaces between drawn contours.

Exercise 2

Do the same as described in Exercise 1, but try and use a different technique, even different-quality paint for each separate element.

Exercise 3

It used to be an essential element of any art-college education to paint a transcription of an old master. It is an excellent discipline. Not only will you come away with a deeper understanding of the artist, but you pick up so many little painterly insights. No other exercise forces you to look at a work of art more closely or more intimately.

Unless you have contacts in high places you will not be allowed for security reasons to do the work directly in the gallery. But if you can choose a work within easy reach of your studio, you could do a good job with the help of several visits and a reproduction. You will derive more benefit if the masterpiece you intend to transcribe is an oil painting, but that is not a hard and fast rule. Try and make it the same size and do a little background research if you can.

Exercise 1

Make a painting using a photograph from a newspaper, a photograph you have taken yourself and a drawing or painting taken directly from life. Treat them technically exactly the same so that you are forced to come to terms with the different problems and possibilities of the different media.

You Angel You *The background figures in this painting were taken from a photograph in the sports pages of a newspaper. An epidiascope was used to project the image onto the top half of the canvas. The angel floating in mid-air is painted from life.*

The head in the foreground was suggested by a family snapshot; the image was too small to project successfully, so I squared it up using a ⅕in (0.5cm) grid of four by eight squares on the photograph and a 6in (15cm) grid of four by eight on the canvas. This only worked partially.

As it was a self-portrait, I set up the bathroom mirrors at right angles to each other in the corner of my studio. This allowed me to go into greater detail as well as giving me a more workable image.

Varnishing

The tendency of artists to varnish their work keeps a sizeable staff of picture restorers in gainful employment at galleries. Rembrandt's *Night Watch* in the Rijksmuseum in Amsterdam was cleaned a few years ago to reveal a vivid daylight scene. The varnish had yellowed and collected so much grime that it resembled a night-time scene.

There are some questions that you must ask yourself before you varnish.

Is the paint thoroughly dry? If it is not, the paint will absorb some of the varnish and it will be more difficult to remove at a later date. Also, the paint will craze, wrinkle or crack in time.

What kind of varnish is being used? Will it discolour with age? The label on the bottle may say that it won't, but do you believe it? Can it be removed from the paint with ease?

Are you sure you want a glossy surface to your painting? Matt varnish is available, but you need to boil it and apply it to your painting hot.

Sometimes if you are using more than one medium with your paint, linseed oil, turpentine and so on, the surface quality will vary from area to area. You can use varnish to unify the image, but a thin glaze of linseed oil or liquin will perform the same function.

I suspect most people varnish their work because it highlights the colours for a time and it makes the picture look nice and new and glossy, like the surface of the dining-room table.

FRAMING AND HANGING

Each picture presents a new problem for framing and I have not always solved the problem satisfactorily.

I have made frames myself, buying a chop saw, getting good-quality timber, learning how to gild and to french polish. After many hours' labour, however, they still look handmade; sometimes this is the quality I am looking for in a frame, but not always.

I have bought frames in junk shops and at antique markets and sales, cleaned them up and made my canvas to fit the frame. This has proved my most successful and economic option. It is, however, becoming increasingly difficult to get the right frame at the right price.

I have gone to various frame shops, but they usually cater for the photography trade and the range of stock they have to suit large paintings is limited. If I am fortunate enough to find the right frame it is usually ridiculously expensive and I resent paying the money.

The real question you have to answer is whether you buy a frame to fit the picture or to fit the surroundings the picture will be hung in. An ornate gilt frame will look out of place in a modern high-tech living room. Similarly, a nice simple handmade pine frame will look out of place round a portrait of the Grand Master of the local Freemason's lodge.

There is only one golden rule to hanging a picture, which is to put the eye-level or horizon at the eye-level of the average standing man (about 5ft 6in (my wife thinks this is sexist, so in our living room I put the eye-level at 4ft 6in). Since I spend most of my time lying down on the settee, the paintings are not right there either, so it is really a matter of personal preference.

Old frames can be painted with spray paint to suit your picture.

The brutal composition of this picture would not have suited a delicate frame. Some industrial timber seemed appropriate. Besides, the painting is 5 × 4ft (152 × 122cm) and proprietary framing at this size is very expensive.

I bought an old frame in a junk shop and stripped off the paint to find it was made of solid oak. I made the canvas to fit the frame.

PAINTINGS TO SEE

The following is a list of paintings on show in British art galleries that are well worth making the pilgrimage to see. I chose them not so much for their place in any art historical pantheon, but for the way the artists use oil paint, which may inform or inspire you.

Visiting large galleries can be a daunting and exhausting business, so much to see and take in. Choose two or three paintings at the most to visit, look at them for at least a quarter of an hour, and for want of a better phrase, 'let it look at you'.

Gaugin *Three Tahitians* (1899) and *Jacob Wrestling with the Angel* (1888), National Gallery of Scotland, Edinburgh.

Faa Ihiehe (1898), Tate Gallery, London.

Bellini *The Doge* (1501), National Gallery, London.

Derain *Barges on the Thames* (1906), City Art Gallery, Leeds.

Cezanne *The Card Players* (1906), Courtauld Institute Gallery, London.

Bathers (1905), National Gallery, London.

Still Life with Teapot (1898), National Gallery of Wales, Cardiff.

Degas *Diego Martelli* (1879), National Gallery of Scotland, Edinburgh.

Young Spartans Exercising (1860), National Gallery, London.

The Rehearsal (1874), City Art Gallery, Glasgow.

Turner *Steamer and Lightship* (c1825–30), *Snow Storm – Steam Boat off a Harbour Mouth* (1842), and *Snow Storm: Hannibal and his Army Crossing the Alps* (1812), Tate Gallery, London.

Caravaggio *The Supper at Emmaus* (1600), National Gallery, London.

Sargent *Ellen Terry* (1889), National Portrait Gallery.

Manet *Bar aux Folies-Bergeres* (1882), Courtauld Institute Gallery, London.

Watteau *Les Plaisirs du Bal* (1719), Dulwich Art Gallery, London.

Poussin *Et in Arcadia Ego* (1630), Chatsworth, Derbyshire.

Hogarth *The Entertainment* (1754), Soane Museum, London.

Raphael *The Bridgewater Madonna* (1507), National Gallery of Scotland, Edinburgh.

Renoir *Le Coup de Vent* (1878), Fitzwilliam Museum, Cambridge.

The Box (1874), The Courtauld Collection, London.

Constable *Dedham Lock and Mill* (c1817), Tate Gallery, London.

Study for the Leaping Horse (1825), Victoria and Albert Museum, London.

Gainsborough *The Morning Walk* (1785), National Gallery, London.

Reynolds *Lord Heathfield* (1787), National Gallery, London.

Portrait of Nelly O'Brien (1763), The Wallace Collection, London.

Frangonard *The Swing* (1766), The Wallace Collection, London.

Rembrandt *Woman Bathing* (1655), National Gallery, London.

Claude Le Lorrain *Landscape with Ascanius Shooting the Stag of Sylvia* (1682), Ashmolean Museum, Oxford.

Madox Brown *Work* (1803), Birmingham City Art Gallery.

Van Gogh *Sunflowers* (1889), Tate Gallery, London.

Monet *Waterlilies* (1916), National Gallery, London.

The Cliff at Fecamp (1881), Aberdeen Art Gallery.

First published in 1992 by
The Crowood Press Ltd
Ramsbury, Marlborough
Wiltshire SN8 2HR

British Library Cataloguing-in-Publication Data

A catalogue record for this book is available from the British Library

ISBN   1 85223 615 9

ACKNOWLEDGEMENTS

I should like to thank the following people who kindly allowed me to reproduce their paintings in this book.

Pete Connors, Jackie Spies, Hannah Ward-Lewis, Nicola Holmes, James Shera, Martin Offiah, Paul Scott, Tom Darden, Mike Brooks, Bob Massey, Geoffrey Kent, Brenda Kent, Glen Smith, Dr Jim Skinner, Carole Ryan, Richard Ryan, Gee Armytage, Anne and Bianca Bounds, Gwyn Roberts, Maureen Stephenson, Jessica Kellogg, Anne and Rebecca Lawrence, Dianne Mills, Wellingborough District Council, Bill and Fiona Donnelly, Minneapolis RFC, Rob Champion, Wilf Scott, Mr A. Nimmo, Alison Otto, Rachel and Gordon Robson, Dean Richards, Richard Hill, Jeremy Guscott, Rory Underwood, Doug Hulme, Dean and Sue Barkley and Darren Garforth.

Photographs by Sue Atkinson
Typeset by Acūté, Stroud, Gloucestershire.
Printed and bound in Great Britain by BPCC Hazells Ltd
Member of BPCC Ltd